MODERN LEADERSHIP

A COMPANION GUIDE FOR TODAY'S LEADERS

Gary Starr

Modern Leadership
A Companion Guide for Today's Leaders

Published by Gary Starr

Copyright © 2018 Gary Starr
All rights reserved.

No part of this publication may be reproduced, stored in a retrieval system, or transmitted in any form or by any means --- electronic, mechanical, photocopy, recording, or any other – without the prior permission of the author.

Amazon ISBN: 9781729460832

Acknowledgments:

I dedicate this book to my wife. I am thankful that God brought you into my life. Your constant love and support through the years have been a rock in my life. May God continue to bless and strengthen our marriage and love for each other.

I also dedicate this book to all of the leaders who I have had the opportunity to learn from. Without the mentoring and leadership of some of you, I would not have been able to become a strong leader.

What you do, work at it with all you heart, as working for the Lord, not for men. Colossians 3:23

Table of Contents

Introduction…………………………..….………1

Leadership Styles……………………...………...8

The New Leader……………………....………..20

Building Relationships as a Leader………...……...44

Communication as a Leader………………..……..52

Respect as a Leader……………………….……72

Coaching as a Leader……………………..……..86

Values as a Leader……………………………..105

Relax as a Leader……………………....…….126

The New Workforce…………………….……..134

Conclusion……………………………….……143

Notes……………………………………….…150

About the Author……………………….……..157

INTRODUCTION

Leadership, a word that everyone recognizes but has so many different meanings and connotations depending on who is speaking. It has the ability to cause a variety of feelings from bliss to anger depending on the experience one has had with those who were placed in a leadership role over them. The Merriam-Webster Dictionary's definition of leadership is; a position as a leader of a group, organization, etc. or the power or ability to lead other people.[1] The sixth President of the United States, John Quincy Adams, stated, " If your actions inspire others to dream more, learn more, do more and become more, you are a leader."[2]

Those may be the official definitions of leadership but just because someone has been placed in a leadership role, does that make them a leader? The second part of the definition is the key, the ability to lead other people. Too often in today's culture, someone in the position of management believes that just because they have been given the title and power, that they are a leader. The Merriam-Webster Dictionary's definition of management is; judicious use of means to accomplish an end or the act or process of deciding how to use something.[3] By definition a manager is not a leader but someone who can take the resources available, be it staff or product and utilize it to accomplish the mission of the organization.

    Those in the position of leadership, in many cases, have not been prepared by mentors or themselves to be able to fulfill the aspects of being a leader. Quite often they have gotten the differences between a manager and a leader confused. Dwight D. Eisenhower said, "Now I think, speaking roughly, by leadership we mean the art of getting someone else to do something that you want done because he wants to do it, not because your position of power can compel him to do it, or your position of authority."[4]

Or General Colin Powell, "Leadership is the art of accomplishing more than the science of management says is possible."[5]

There are plenty of people who are managers officially or unofficially that are good at managing. A good manager knows how to follow procedure and routines and make accurate calculations and statistics based on the resources available. They can make employee schedules, maintain inventories and plan for the future based on previous outcomes. There are so many examples recently of large companies installing a new CEO into their company only to have that CEO ultimately leave the company in no better and usually worse condition than when they arrived. Many of these CEOs were recognized because of their great management abilities but unfortunately they did not know how to lead well. In order to produce great results, a person needs to be able to manage but more importantly be able to lead. "Management is the production of acceptable results with known constraints….Leadership is changing the order of things….Only leaders can drive change."[6] Peter Drucker, a respected business consultant, compares the differences between management and leadership in his writings. He defines leadership as, "Leadership is the lifting of a man's vision to higher sights, the raising of a man's performance to a higher standard, the building of a man's personality beyond its normal limitations."[7]

The title or position of leader has taken on the connotation of mistrust as CEO's pad their wallets at the expense of their staff, Congress pad their wallets at the expense of their constituents and many in positions of leadership end up in the news for every unimaginable, questionable and illegal action. Leaders are no longer viewed as someone that are looking out for the benefit of the whole group. The average citizen would not deny a person the ability to make money based on their position or talents but they are angry about recent greed because leaders are doing it at the expense of their staff and the public and not protecting them. These perceptions have caused many businesses and organizations to falter and not reach their full potential as employees never feel the need to perform for a lackluster leader. Leaders looking to benefit and enjoy perks solely for their own gain have learned that employees actually have the power to push those type of leaders out of their position by not performing.

The purpose of this book is to define what it takes to be a dynamic exceptional leader in the 21st Century. The style of leadership that worked 10 or 20 years ago no longer works in a majority of the environments. Everyone at all stages of experience, from the aspiring leader to the seasoned leader, will benefit from reading this book. You have an opportunity to make yourself stand out as a strong leader in a world where strong leaders are lacking and seem to be going extinct. Former GE CEO Jack Welch had the right idea twenty plus years ago when he stated, "The world of the 1990's and beyond will not belong to 'managers' or those who can make the numbers dance. The world will belong to passionate, driven leaders – people who not only have enormous amounts of energy but who can energize those whom they lead."[8]

Companies such as Disney with strong historical leadership are referred to a lot in this book. Disney is a company that many try to emulate even to the point Disney has a training program for leaders that do not work for Disney. Many would overlook the U.S. military as prime example of strong leadership but even retired legendary leader at Disney, Lee Cockerell states that the U.S. Army is constantly adapting and training leaders at every level.

I have written this book as though I was sitting next to you discussing the aspects of leadership. The hope is to ensure that you will enjoy reading and learning how to become a better leader. It isn't your typical book written from a statistical point of view, even though there will be some statistics, or from an academic point of view. The idea is to make it more relatable and readable.

LEADERSHIP STYLES

Individuals find themselves in the position of leadership through different paths ranging from inheriting a position to being promoted. Some aspire to a leadership position for their own personal advancement, others for the benefit of the group and some never aspired or expected to be in a leadership role. While none of these methods are wrong, they all have one thing in common, the person placed in a leadership role now has to decide what style of leader they are going to be. The style of leader a person chooses to be will dictate how well they will be respected and followed by others. Depending on what resource you look at, the length of the list and styles of leaders differs. One thing is standard though, there are certain styles of leadership that just makes bad leaders. You will want to avoid those styles of leadership but the question arises is there a single best style of leadership. My answer would be yes, but none of the previous classifications or standards of leadership work in the 21st century and most likely won't work in the future. As the workforce continues to move towards more intellectual and mind-based jobs versus manual labor, leadership styles will need to continue to change and keep up with employee demands and needs.

There are about 10 style of leadership that have been identified over the past 10 – 20 years, depending on which book or study you read there might be more or less styles listed. More were used in your parent's or grandparen'ts era with only a few still having any merits that can be utilized in the 21st century. I've listed them here for information purposes only because the rest of the book will address necessary leadership qualities for the 21st century.

1. Laissez-Faire – this leader lacks direct supervision of employees. This leader has been placed into a

leadership role most likely before they were prepared or against their will. They have strong friendships with their staff and are afraid to assert leadership for fear of losing those friendships. Thus the staff are left to act on their own accord and without direction or leadership.

2. Autocratic – this leader makes decisions without the input of others. This leader wants to assert their authority to ensure all staff know who is boss. A new leader can be like this at times, believing this the only way to get staff to follow while trying to impress their superior. Leaders with strong egos can fall within this group as well.

3. Participative – this leader has a democratic style, encouraging input from all members of the team. A problem that arises with this style is that a lot of

listening is required by the leader and there is a risk that very little will get done particularly in large teams.

4. Transactional – this leader rewards or punishes based on goals. This may be more a management style based on the earlier definition of management.
5. Transformational – this leader motivates staff to enhance productivity and efficiency through communication and remains highly visibility. One of the styles that can be incorporated in the 21st century leader.
6. Charismatic – this leader influences others to do something through the power of their personality. A great example of a positive recent charismatic leader is President Bill Clinton but there are negative charismatic leaders with Hitler as an example.

7. Command & Control – this leader follows the rules and expects others to do the same. A prime example of this style of leader would be in the military but can be found everywhere as well.
8. Pace Setter – this leader sets high goals for self and the group. The team must already be motivated and successful for this style to work. If this style is maintained for a long period of time there is a potential for burn-out and team turnover. Although if properly controlled, it too can be incorporated in the 21st century leader.
9. Servant – this leader wants to help others succeed before self. The leader typically is not in the forefront and seldom takes the credit for the achievement of the group. This style will be discussed as a strong trait of the 21st century leader.

10. Situational – this leader gives direction and support while empowering and coaching their staff. Again another style that can find pieces being incorporated in the 21st century leader.

Before progressing, you should take a moment and self-evaluate what type of leader you currently are and what leadership style you possess. Be honest with yourself. The type of leader I was 20 years ago is different than the leader I am today. It is all about growth and learning to be the best leader you can be and I still learn new things every day. Look at the list of leadership styles and write down the style that you feel best corresponds to you. Next look at the below chart and circle the descriptions that relate to how you perceive yourself as a leader.

Connect With Staff	Disconnected With Staff
Present and Accessible	Distant and Unapproachable
Communication is Wide Open	There is No Communication

Share Your Knowledge	Leave Staff to Fend for Themselves
Praise, Encourage, Recognize, Thank	Demanding and Critical
Staff Feel Relaxed and Free	Staff Feel Oppressed

If you feel brave and comfortable, at this stage you could always ask your staff to do the same exercise concerning what type of leader you are. Chances are that you look at what you picked and your current work environment and realize that these styles are antiquated and won't work successfully in the 21st century. "Doing things the old way, does not open new doors" – Unknown. Without change and growth personally, your staff and company will not be able to grow and compete in the ever changing economy. So throw out your ideas of what it means to be a leader and prepare to become a great leader. And remember, the learning process never ends. The best leaders continue to read books written by or about strong leaders and digest how they became recognized as strong leaders. As John F. Kennedy said, "Leadership and learning are indispensable to each other."[9]

Companies that aren't adapting to the change in employee relation dynamics are seeing higher turnover rates and their companies are stagnating and even worse, going out of business. I've witnessed people taking lower salaries to work for a company that allows them to use their talents to their fullest and even people that embrace unemployment as a salvation from working for a company that only saw them as an object or number in the bottom line. This mentality is costing companies money in hiring and training even though this is an area they should be able to control and manage as the easiest of all monetary losses. Worker satisfaction and commitment to employers in America is at an all-time low. Gallup estimates it costs $300 billion in lost productivity.[10] Corporate America and the civilian sector may not think of the U.S. Military as an example to follow when it comes to leadership because they don't understand or comprehend it, but the opposite is true. During World War II General Patton stated, "Percepts used by the military are, have always been, and will always be a good way to conduct business. Professionalism, pragmatism, discipline, and definition and constancy of purpose will never go out of style."[11] And things have not changed in 70 years when Lt. General George J. Flynn wrote, "These organizations have strong cultures and shared values, understand the importance of team work, create trust among their member, maintain focus, and most important, understand the importance of people and relationships to their mission success."[12]

Leaders of the 21st century need to stop learning the leadership styles of the past 30 years which were primarily leader - follower and embrace a new style that empowers everyone to be a potential leader. Lee Cockerell writes, "As we say at Disney, "In times of drastic change, it is the learners who inherit the future."[13] The U.S. military is and has been a great example of this through the ages. The U.S. military is constructed so that if in the time of war if the leader is incapacitated the mission keeps moving forward and is accomplished because the next highest ranking person takes over and this can keep happening until there is no one left. One of the cold war strategies if we were ever to go to war with the Soviet Union was to take out the leadership because unlike the U.S. military, they would not be able to keep functioning because staff weren't empowered to take over. You also hear this often in football where a starter gets hurt and the "next man up" fills the position without hindrance to the team's abilities. I have always said to the horror of chuckle of others that I've trained someone to replace me in case I am hit by a bus on the way home. It is important to train the next person and selfish to hoard knowledge. Always set high standards for yourself and others and hold yourself accountable. Serve as the role model of training the next leader to replace you.

Does this mean leaders should have a leadership style of laissez-faire then where there is a lack of direction given? No, the leader is still an important integrate part of a company or organization. The leader must assume a new role and image though. The leadership styles of participative (democratic style, encouraging input from all members of the team) and situational (gives direction and support while empowering and coaching their staff) must be adapted and cultivated from the CEO down to the newest hire. Leaders can no longer sit on the sideline barking orders and must get in the game and achieve to become the best leader there is. "Leadership is the challenge to be something more than average." ~ Jim Rohn

So what is the first step in becoming a strong leader in the 21st century? Self-awareness. What kind of leader are you? Are you hands on, working side by side with your staff or are you hiding in your office dispersing orders of what needs to be done while at the same time stifling your staff ability to utilize their talents while you micro-manage? "Leadership is a demanding, noble discipline not to be entered into frivolously or casually," according to the authors of The Truth About Leadership.[14]

THE NEW LEADER

I'm sure you have worked for many managers, some were weak managers and poor leaders, some were good managers but poor leaders and some were good managers and good leaders. I have years of experience in different types of management roles and will admit I have been a poor leader but have grown to be a good leader. All leaders start with very little experience and make mistakes but the ability and willingness to learn from the mistakes helps one to become a great leader later. If you are a young leader, hopefully you have a strong leader to learn from and if you don't, find one. In fact if you have someone that you feel would be a good mentor, you may want to work through this book together and have them hold you accountable for growing as a leader.

So, are good leaders born or created? Depending on who you listen to or what you read, the argument can go either way. I personally believe good leaders are created but some of the necessary traits needed, a person is born with. The environment that someone grows up in (good or bad) and their own personal drive to succeed, play a larger role as to whether someone can be trained to be a good leader. Martin Luther King Jr. is considered to be one of the 20th century's best leaders yet he was born in a monetarily poor environment, but his upbringing among family church leaders and mentors created a rich environment to birth a strong leader. Add his personal drive to succeed and learn, and you end up with a strong leader. On the other hand, there are those who were born with the proverbial silver spoon in their mouth and in an environment that should create a strong leader but they end up being a poor leader due that environment or the unwillingness to learn how to become a strong leader. I am not going to list a specific example but each of you can probably think of a big company CEO, President or politician that fits this example.

The good news is that as a young manager receiving their first position or a seasoned manager starting a new a position, you have a fresh start and the ability to dictate what kind of leader you will be. Those who have held leadership roles before need to remember that every time they change positions and accept a new leadership role, they are essentially starting over as a leader with a new set of staff. It just won't take as long to get up and running as a strong leader due to your previous leadership experiences.

The first question, you need to ask yourself though, is why do you want to assume a management role with the leadership responsibilities that come with it. Your answer will dictate how successful you will become as a leader. Many of us, including myself, when we are young in years, strive to become managers for several reasons; increase in pay, perception of less work, power, ego, influence over others, the perceived notion that we think we know everything. Or was it because you wanted to be a servant leader to your staff. What many find out quickly is that their first leadership position comes with none of the perceived benefits and can quickly feel like an anchor around your neck pulling you down to the dark depths of despair. It turns out that just because you have been given a leadership position, it doesn't mean people immediately have to respect you or your authority. If you have ever been in the military, you can relate to the saying, "I may have to salute and respect your rank but it doesn't mean I have to respect you." Just because you have been given a position or title doesn't mean you have arrived.

Notice, I use the word "given" your leadership position. Leadership is a privilege and a good leader knows that there is more to it than just the position and title. Lt. General George J. Flynn states, "Great leaders truly care about those they are privileged to lead and understand that the true cost of the leadership privilege comes at the expense of self-interest."[15] A leader receives their position if done properly based on their potential to lead and not based on birth-right, politics, seniority or convenience. You have been given your leadership position so what are you going to do with it? A good leader quickly recognizes that they have been given a responsibility for the well-being of the company and their staff. This is not your parent's or grandparent's era style of leadership, the concept of leading with an iron fist in the Command and Control style doesn't fit in the 21st Century for the most part. Those who strived to become leaders for the power and their ego will quickly fail as leaders because they now have authority but no respect from their staff.

You can demand action from your staff but you can't demand their respect, it has to be earned.

Leaders need to understand that power is a two-sided coin; the power they perceive they have and on the other side the power followers desire from or are willing to concede to the leader.[16] Dwight D. Eisenhower also remarked in the same speech as previously annotated; "A commander of a regiment is not necessarily a leader. He has all the appurtenances of power given by a set of Army regulations by which he can compel unified action. He can say to a body such as this, "Rise," and "Sit down." You do it exactly. But that is not a leader."[17] Corporate America is no different. Someone can be promoted to a management position at any level including CEO and they can command action but the title does not make them a leader. And that is why companies falter and struggle. The current management structure believes they can just lead by coercion.

"You can assign a man to a leadership position, but no one will ever really be a leader until his appointment is ratified in the hearts and minds of his soldiers." ~ General William Livsey[18]

The question then becomes, what are you going to do to earn the hearts and minds of your staff? Self-assessment of who you are and reaching out to successful leaders should be one of your first priorities. You have heard the saying, "You don't know what you don't know." So you need to quickly check your ego because you may have gotten your position on your own accomplishments but you are quickly going to learn that the tables are shifted to your staff. Without their support and respect, you will not progress any further on the leadership ladder. Part of your self-assessment should be what you think your weaknesses and strengths are, what are your values, what are your potential pitfalls or bad habits, and what are your goals for yourself and your staff. Captain Mike Abrashoff took a struggling submarine crew and guided them to become the best, in his book *It's Your Ship*, "In a nutshell hard experience has taught me that real leadership is about understanding yourself first, then using that to create a superb organization. Leaders must free their staff to fulfill their talents to the utmost. However, most obstacles that limit people's potential are set in motion by the leader and are rooted in his or her own fears, ego needs and unproductive habits. When leaders explore deep within their thoughts and feelings in order to understand themselves, a transformation can take shape."[19]

    Real influence and power of leaders does not come from their job title. Anybody can print a business card with any title they want to bestow on themselves. The same can be seen in e-mail signatures, which are loaded with titles that really mean nothing expect to stroke the ego of the person using the title. Many times these inflated titles are given to justify perks associated with elevated positions and self gain. Staff and the public are not stupid and see right through someone with a title that has no knowledge or ability in their position. It is not uncommon to see the best leaders in a company without inflated job titles and performing more than one function. They walk the walk and talk the talk as leaders which is the true power of a leader which staff respect. "Never let your ego get so close to your position that when your position goes, your ego goes with it."[20]

Values play a large role in successfully gaining the respect of your staff. Your values dictate your behavior and this in turn is what your staff sees and assesses when deciding whether they will follow you or not. If your staff senses that your values are aligned with your own self gain and doesn't include their well-being then your success as a leader has been eliminated. The biggest trait that your staff will value in you according to surveys is your ability to lead by example. Again, just because you have been given a position or title doesn't mean you have made it and you can now just sit back and partake in the perceived benefits that come with your position. I am sure that you can remember, without thinking too hard, a manager you have had in the past that you resented because they thought just because they had a position and title, they didn't have to do anything. If you didn't appreciate how you felt with a leader like that then you shouldn't want to duplicate that style. As a leader you must remember the golden rule we were all taught as a child, "Do to others as you would want them to do to you." Lead by example and your staff will respect you not just your position but you and will follow you. An ancient example of this would be King Arthur and his knights. King Arthur created a round table to symbolize that everyone who sat at it had an equal ability to participate. Although he was king, he led by example.

You need to personally think that you can and will make a difference. Every interview I've had for a leadership position, I've always been asked what kind of leader are you? My answer has and always will be, "I can get anyone to jump off a bridge with me, not for me." I observed and learned this from leaders I had while in the U.S. Army. General Patton wrote, "It's the job of the commander to lead his soldiers. It's his job to be in the front lines where the shooting is taking place. If you can't accept responsibility, requirements, and inherent danger of command, get the hell out."[21] In a knowledge based employee environment, a leader has to prove they know what they are talking about and doing. Getting a degree, receiving a management position because of it and giving orders no longer works in this world where every piece of information is available to anyone through a quick search on the internet. You have to earn the respect of your staff and the only way to do that is to walk the walk. I had a manager who received a MBA (we referred to the MBA as Master Bullshit Artist) because he could talk a good talk and was hired as the director of the IT department primarily because of the degree, but he had very little knowledge of how IT worked. He was learning on the job and making decisions on his own without consulting those who were his staff and more experienced. Our department never reached its full potential because he was not leading and did not have the loyalty of his staff. Effective leaders are constantly pointing their team in the direction they are heading and explaining why it is beneficial to everyone to be heading in that same direction.

So why and where should you be leading your staff? Remember an aspect of leadership is to get someone to do something because they want to, not because you ordered it. Do you think a soldier would blindly follow orders to take an objective with bullets flying past them with the potential of death if they didn't have a squad leader who was leading the way and taking the same risks? The squad leader in this case is taking his soldiers somewhere to achieve a goal. When leaders don't have a goal to lead their staff to, everyone becomes stagnant and objectives are not achieved. At one of my retail management positions, I was able to be more successful at getting the store cleaned up at closing each night than other managers. The reason was because every person working when I closed knew that I was not afraid to get my hands dirty and help out instead of just sitting in the office. I led by example and my staff respected me for that and they started to help other areas of the store when their departments were finished, not because I asked them to, but because they wanted to.

    Another key value that a lot of new leaders fall prey to is the sense of entitlements of being a leader. Examples of entitlement include but not inclusive can be; not getting your hands dirty, sitting around in your office, doing unproductive functions on your computer, extended lunches, arriving late or leaving early, and/or any other thing that comes to mind that would make a leader feel important. We all have witnessed leaders like this and the feelings and thoughts we had concerning the issue. It is a fast way to alienate and again lose the respect of your staff. Leaders that have a position and title but do not wave it around to increase their sense of importance, are leaders that are respected in society the most. In a world that embraces everyone looking out for themselves and inflated egos, this can be a tough area to avoid temptation. You have to be honest with yourself and ask if a particular entitlement is the right thing to do? Just because you have a right to do something doesn't make it right. Just look at the collapse recently of so many CEOs.

CEOs are quickly learning as more and more are being fired that they are replaceable and that their position is only temporary, that the position is a privilege, not a right. The position requires more than you can offer on your own and that they have been given stewardship of the company not ownership. Former Goldman Sachs Chief Executive, Greg Smith realized this and as he was heading out the door he wrote, "The firm changed the way it thought about leadership. Leadership used to be about ideas, setting an example and doing the right thing. Today, if you make enough money for the firm (and are not currently an axe murderer) you will be promoted into a position of influence."[22] No one would begrudge those in leadership of extra perks and pay but the problem arises when someone's primary reason to hold a position is solely for their own personal gain and not the betterment of the company or their staff.

    As a new leader, you need to be very careful of your viewpoint of your staff. If you were promoted from the ranks, then those who were your friends and equals have now been placed under your leadership and authority. This scenario tends to trip up new leaders quite often. One day you are joking around in the break room and the next you are expected to possibly discipline that same person. As humans we tend to make a drastic change in our thinking and change our viewpoint of our staff as cogs in the system, become distant emotionally and attempt to throw around our new given authority. The new title and position become the most important things in our minds. If you allow this type of attitude to occur, your staff, in your eyes will become a nuisance and are only an obstacle to you being able to do your job and get ahead. You will no longer see your staff as human beings. Your staff will quickly figure out that you don't care about their well-being and you will lose the ability to get them to do things because they want to. You will lose their respect and it takes more effort to regain someone's respect after you have lost it. T.S. Elliot wrote, "Half of the harm that is done in this world is due to people who want to feel important… They do not mean to do harm… They are absorbed in the endless struggle to think well of themselves."[23]

Another pitfall to avoid as a new leader, which is prevalent in many companies, is the "us versus them" mentality. These type of leaders attempt to hoard resources for their own departments, create separation between departments and attempt to create their own little world of dominance. This is a true sign of weakness in a leader. You need to feel confident enough that your staff will work with other departments productively and that the sharing of ideas will benefit everyone. I read a good example of this concerning the invention of the post-it note by 3M. One department created the stickiness but it didn't meet the requirements for what their project needed so it was filed away. But at 3M the open sharing of ideas is encouraged and required so when another department was looking for a solution to their project, the formula for the right amount of stickiness was already completed by the first department. This type of thinking benefits everyone involved including the company, staff and leaders. As Walt Disney stated, "Whatever we accomplish belongs to our entire group, a tribute to our combined effort."[24]

    Let's take a quick synopsis of what you have read so far in this chapter. Positions and titles are given and it doesn't mean you have arrived but instead it is a privilege to lead others. You have a responsibility to the company and others. You aren't ratified as a leader until your staff says you earned it. Your values will dictate your actions and your ability to gain the respect of your staff. Being a leader is measured by your staff performing because they want to. Entitlements of leadership can be entrapments that undermine the respect of your staff. Trusting your staff to work across departmental lines benefits everyone including you.

So, what is the recurring theme so far? The position you hold is not about you but about others, particularly your staff. Someone saw your potential to lead others and gave you an opportunity. But, are you going to succeed without your staff? No! In fact, if you want to move up the chain of command and higher leadership positions, you will need to take your staff with you. They may not actually move to a new department when you get promoted but when you do leave the department, the staff will be at a higher level of accomplishment and production. A famous quote of Zig Ziglar is, "You can have everything in life you want, if you will just help enough other people get what they want."[25]

Remember earlier I mentioned that leadership requires action and these actions are taking others with you as you climb the hill and having them climb that hill because they want to, not because you ordered it. Your staff will be a deciding factor as to whether you successfully move from the lowest level of leadership. They can work with you for success or they can sabotage the success of the company and ultimately your ability to remain employed let alone move up in leadership. "The test of a leader lies in the reaction and response of his followers. He should not have to impose authority. Bossiness, in itself, never made a leader. He must make his influence felt by example and the instilling of confidence in his followers. The greatness of a leader is measured by the achievements of the led. This is the ultimate test of his effectiveness." – General Omar Bradley[26] The leader – follower leadership style of from 10 – 20 years ago is no longer effective or will work in the 21st century. As a leader, your staff will expect you to walk along beside them and to look out for their best interests along the journey.

Failure to embrace this concept will result in staff that will not work at their best. No one wants to work for someone that is only looking out for their own well-being at the expense of everyone else. They will be willing, however, to give their all to someone they respect, trust and know will look out for everyone's well-being. Take a quick assessment of those that work around you. Which department has staff that watch the clock and are out the door as fast as their legs will move at the end of the day? Which department is walking around unconcerned about the quality of work or even say what everyone has heard, "Good enough for government work?" What department has a bunch of people sitting or walking around looking like zombies, are constantly making the same mistakes or are unengaged? Which department has a high turnover of staff? That department has a weak leader and if it is your department and you are the leader, you have some work to do. When people are asked why they leave a company, it is because of personality conflicts and typically the leader they work for. The company is just an entity but a leader has the ability to affect how their staff feel and act.

You are ultimately responsible for your own success or failure as a leader but just as a baby requires nourishment, direction and guidance to grow so does a new leader. I will discuss the responsibilities of an experienced leader to train future leaders later in the book but I want to address it slightly here. A staff member has been pinpointed for a possible management position due to their abilities to manage and their job performance. But do they have leadership abilities and what have you or the company done to prepare them for promotion? Companies and superiors are dropping the ball on training and preparing future leaders for the most part. This is for multiple reasons such as the company doesn't want to spend the money, which can cost more in the long run, doesn't understand the difference between management and leadership or a superior who feels threatened or thinks they are unreplaceable. This sets the newly promoted leader up for failure or as some like to say "sink or swim".

Companies don't realize that this mentality will actually cost the company more money over the long run. An unprepared leader will take longer to get their team functioning and performing the company mission, will cause moral issues as the team struggles and will create high turnover, thus needing to train new employees and the cost of replacing the new leader when they don't succeed. Superiors also need to understand the benefit of training their replacement. It is human nature, particularly in this current economic environment, to try to protect your position by not sharing information and trying to make yourself irreplaceable. This thought process actually has negative impacts on the superior such as, preventing promotion because there isn't someone to fill their current position, having to be overworked because no one else can assist with duties or a disruption in work production during vacations or extended medical leaves. I like to ask people, "What if you were hit by a bus tonight, would work flow be able to continue uninterrupted?"

As a new leader, if you are not receiving the support that you think you require to succeed, don't be afraid to ask an experienced leader for guidance and assistance. Depending on your environment, you may not receive the assistance you need, so take responsibility for your growth and make sure you read and study as many resources as possible. There is no excuse not to find leadership resources since the internet contains more at your fingertips than you will ever have time to read and digest.

BUILDING RELATIONSHIPS AS A LEADER

Relationships are key in being a leader, no matter if you are a new or an experienced leader. The attitude of the past 10 – 20 years leaders have been distant from their staff, sitting in the office with the door closed, will no longer work in the 21st century. After World War I and World War II we saw an unbelievable business growth in the United States and this was because the worker felt as though their workplace was family and they took pride in what they were producing. That started to change in the 1970's and particularly the 1980's as leaders lost focus of what was important and instead money and perks became their central focus. The American workforce began to become disgruntled and feel as though they are only treated as objects or as a cog in the company. Employees and staff were no longer thought of as humans but as dollar signs. This mentality has stifled the growth of strong leadership in most companies.

There are few companies that have not fallen into this trap and they are refocusing the importance of taking care of their employees and now those companies are succeeding.

Your position in leadership will not get your staff to perform. "The truth is that if you have to tell people that you're the leader, you're not."[27] Forming relationships with your staff should be a primary goal from the start. I'm not talking about having a friendship outside of work where you are all drinking at the bar or sitting around watching the football game but a relationship where you know who your staff are and what is important to them. Are they married, how many kids they have, what are their aspirations and goals, their hobbies, what they did on the weekend. You have to be sincere too because your staff will be able to pick-up quickly if you are truly sincere about getting to know them or not. In order to be a good leader you have to like people.

I have had the pleasure of hearing Rudy Giuliani, former Mayor of NYC, speak on leadership. One statement that he always makes is, "It's more important to go to a funeral than a wedding. You have to be there when things go wrong." It meant more to his staff and staff that they knew their leader was there to support them no matter the circumstances particularly when things were rough. Lee Cockerell agrees, "They hire the right people, train them, trust them, respect them, listen to them, and sure to be there for them when needed."[28] The key is as a leader you have to be sincere that you care about your staff because if you are not, it will be detrimental to your ability to lead. At one employer I worked for, we would have a departmental meeting every Monday. The department head would start the meeting asking us how our weekends went and we would all share what we did and how they went. It would appear that the department head truly was interested in his staff but it quickly became apparent that he wasn't truly listening to anything we shared. Because as the day went on, he would ask everyone again how their weekend went or acted surprised when 2 of us were discussing further about our weekend. Which leader got more from their staff, Rudy Giuliani or the manager I had?

 If you want to be a leader, are one or have been one, you most likely have been influencing others by the relationship you have with them from the time you were born. Sometimes these relationships have led you to be a leader for either good or bad and you didn't even realize it. Take a look at your childhood and the friends you had or even your siblings, particularly if you have younger siblings. Did you dictate what game would be played, which television show would be watched, created a club or group or who would be responsible for certain jobs? Your relationship with these individuals influenced how they viewed and respected you. The same principals occur now that you are an adult, only now you have adult staff that are wiser, more cynical, and have more needs and responsibilities. As a leader you aren't going to be able to control how your staff is going to respond to you but you are able to influence it by the way you treat your staff.

Building relationships is a difficult venture for many people in the 21st century due to the changes in our culture. Neighborhoods used to be where everyone knew and talked to each other on a daily basis but now most people couldn't even tell you their neighbor's name. Kids used to play outside with each other but now can play the same video game with each other without even leaving their home. Current technology such as e-mail, texting, apps, social media and the internet have widened the gap of human interaction and have made it easier for people to avoid having a face to face relationship which requires more work to create and maintain. Developing relationship skills though are necessary to develop an understanding of oneself, how to interact with others and to succeed in the workforce.

Do you know yourself and are you comfortable in your own skin? Your self-image has been dictated by your experiences with others in life such as parents; friends, teachers, co-workers and strangers. You have to like yourself before you can like others, including your staff, otherwise you will sabotage unknowingly or on purpose, their success in order to increase your self-image. I think many people including myself, have gone through this at some point in their early stages of growth as a leader. The problem are those who don't do a self-assessment regularly or are unable to recognize their deflated self-worth for one reason or another. These leaders will quickly find themselves out of a position or job and those who maintain their jobs will never be successful at getting their staff to produce at their highest abilities.

Young leaders may find it difficult to assess their staff and the reactions they experience when it comes to a relationship with them or between staff members. The awesome thing about humans is that we are all different but at the same time this can be frustrating and tough to navigate. Everyone reacts different to circumstances and the environment around them. One of things concerning relationships with your staff that probably will take the longest to master, is the ability to understand how each individual will react to you based on a particular circumstance. Overreaction or feeling personally hurt is a natural response when a staff member reacts in way we don't want or expect. Being a leader at times requires thick skin and the ability to respond appropriately to every circumstance. I don't know of any leader that is perfect at this all of the time but even how you respond to your failure to act properly will dictate how your staff reacts and respects you in the future.

You as the leader have the responsibility and ability to control how relationships develop between you and your staff and between your staff members. As a leader you have to eliminate the dynamic where people are dragging each other down but instead you should be leading the charge of raising everyone up. Your positive relationship example will increase your ability to get your staff to work at their highest potential and it will multiply itself as they replicate your actions with each other, with the rest of the company, your customers and even in their personal lives at home.

COMMUNICATION AS A LEADER

Now that you understand the importance of having positive strong relationships, you will be able to communicate with your staff more effectively. As a leader you will not be able to get your staff to accomplish anything without good communication and a strong leader understands that communication is a two way street. The ability to communicate is the leader's most effective tool and foundation to be able to lead effectively. The stronger your communication skills the more your staff will respect you and will perform at their highest level because they want to. Strong communication requires a leader to open themselves to perceived risk at times but in reality the rewards are numerous and it is a bigger risk not to communicate effectively. Communication is Rudy Giuliani's fifth principle of leadership because you need to be able to get what you want from them.[29] Everyone I'm sure has heard, when someone is asked in a company what is going on, "I don't know, they keep us in the dark like mushrooms and feed us a bunch of manure." In order for your staff to understand what you are trying to accomplish and for them to feel a viable part of the company they need to be and feel informed. I had a staff member who was a part of a company for 20+ years say that I was the best manager he had ever had. It was simply because I kept him informed unlike any previous manager. Communication has to be a daily function because there is always something that can be relayed or discussed. These communications must have value, consistent tone and you must know why you are communicating. Are you explaining something, overcoming objection, selling or persuading, celebrating or entertaining.[30]

What is the number one way in business to disseminate information? Yep, the dreaded meeting. Meetings in corporate America are held every day, needed or not and most people would argue that the last meeting they went to was not needed. Most meetings are a part of the old way of leading of top down managing. A majority of the time a manager of a particular group leads the meeting and dictates stats about performance, mentions issues that have arisen, passes along what their superior wants accomplished and any other informational filler. If there is any solicitation to the group for feedback or ideas, it is usually isn't a sincere gesture because the leader is going to demand their way be the course of action. These meetings create employees that are void of intellectual thinking and don't feel a part of the company. Too many and extensively long meetings are a symptom of a flawed structure. Instead meetings should be a productive time where the whole team can provide ideas and solutions and not every issue needs to be solved immediately. Use this time to give your staff the ultimate goal that needs to be achieved and let them come up with the methods to achieve it. "The ability to create a clear and powerful vision of a desired outcome is an indispensable element of success for the Top Performance Leader."[31] Your staff need to feel as though they have a stake in the success of the company.

You still need to be involved and guide but be leery of taking total control. Competent, intellectually engaged staff will amaze you how they will succeed to excellence in accomplishing a goal. Listening is a part of communication and leadership as well. Listen to your employees and they will tell you where things are going well and where things aren't. "The task of leadership is not to put greatness into people, but to elicit it, for the greatness is there already." ~John Buchan. More often than not leaders believe that their staff have nothing to share but the opposite is quite true. Listening with open unfiltered ears will improve your leadership abilities and enable you to act appropriately. Have you ever wondered why veterans of the military think highly of their time in the service and miss it? It is not because they like to take orders but because in the military they knew why they were running in the direction of the bullets while in the civilian world most employees have no clue why they are moving in a particular direction. One final point to drive home the importance of this, "…it becomes increasingly important that everyone throughout the organization understands what the organization is about."[32] As a leader you must be communicate clearly and with purpose at all times.

So, the first step to communication is not speaking but to listen. Communication is literally a two-way street just like you have heard so many times. Your staff will direct you towards where there are potential improvements, where the pitfalls are, and new ideas. They are on the front line every day and have firsthand experience of what it takes to get the job done in the most effective and profitable way. Ask your staff questions to find out what they think or feel. Too often leaders are too quick to start barking orders on how to accomplish the needed tasks based only on their rudimentary knowledge derived from policies and manuals written by people that only performed the task a few times. What works in a best case laboratory test setting typically won't cover every issue that can and will occur for a task. When I was in the Army and graduated from AIT (Advance Individual Training), the first thing I was told at my first assignment was to forget just about everything I learned in the training because real world experience would require different actions than what the laboratory or classroom taught.

Good communication requires a connection between both parties and if done properly communication will lead to a stronger team, production increases and your leadership will be more effective. Your staff will be more open to your influence and leadership if they feel as though they have a strong connection with you. Good communication also grows respect, a reoccurring aspect of being a good leader. Remember, as a leader in the 21st century you cannot move ahead in your career without the support of your staff. The *Harvard Business Review* wrote, "The number one criteria for advancement and promotion for professionals is an ability to communicate effectively."[33] Just take a look at many of the job postings and one recurring theme no matter the type of position is the need to be able to communicate effectively.

Leadership requires the ability to get your staff to understand the vision that you and the company have. The only way to accomplish that is through good communication. Too often I ask people what their company's vision is and they can't explain it. How do you expect your staff to know which direction to head and what is expected of them if it has not been communicated to them in a way that they understand? Besides understanding the vision, you need to communicate in a way that relates to your staff and that they are willing to buy into it. Everybody is different and those in different position or levels of their careers need things explained to them differently. Take for example those who work in the accounting office or your IT techs. Just ask any company with an IT staff and you will probably hear the frustration that the techs have their own language and it is hard to understand what they are saying. Never assume that just because the leadership understands and comprehends the vision and direction of the company based on what has been communicated that everyone in the company understands.

In *Turn the Ship Around,* Capt. Marquet had a system to maintain control and at the same time give vision and feedback to his crew through good communication with short conversations early in any project. "Short, early conversations is a mechanism for control. It is a mechanism for control because the conversations did not consist of me telling them what to do. They were opportunities for the crew to get early feedback, on how they were tackling problems. This allowed them to retain control of the solution. These early, guided discussions, also provided clarity to the crew about what we wanted to accomplish. Many lasted only thirty seconds, but they saved hours of time."[34] I'm sure you have had that leader that thinks talking continuously is the proper way to communicate while everyone around them start to roll their eyes, check their watches or start nodding off. But if you look at the quotes of the most successful leaders, they are only a sentence or two. Being direct and precise when communicating has a greater effect on all parties and more is retained and acted upon. Jack Welch agrees with this thought, "You can't believe how hard it is for people to be simple, how much they fear being simple. They worry if they're simple, people will think they're simpleminded. In reality, of course, it's just the reverse. Clear, tough-minded people are the most simple."[35]

Don't be afraid of having after action reviews when a project is completed. It is a great form of communication because those who were directly involved in the project get to give feedback of what they directly observed or performed thus making them feel they have a stake in how future projects will be conducted. The key to make these work though is to include staff from all levels, not just management. Too often companies overlook the experience of those who are actually performing the actions and have hands on experience to what was successful and what could use improvement. Those in management positions do not witness all aspects of a project thus they can't give the best perspectives of the step by step portions of the project since they are only focused on the final outcome. Be sure to share the final report with everyone involved so that again, they realize their contributions were appreciated and that they have a stake in the success of the company.

Another part of good communication is being up front and honest with people. Quite often in our society it has become an acceptable practice to tell a little white lie or sugar coat things when speaking with others or answering questions. The problem with this is that it only damages your integrity, relationship and respect from your staff. Companies tend to communicate only good news to its staff due to the fear that bad news will erode moral and work production. I'm not saying that every piece of bad news needs to be communicated to everyone but the pieces that won't affect the public company image or secrets should be shared. You would be surprised that your staff probably senses or knows more already about the bad news than you think. By not addressing it head on, you will only open the possibility of the talk among the staff, which could fester and grow into assumptions that are untrue, causing a disruption in productivity and moral. Don't be afraid of sharing bad news, it is an opportunity to open the door of communication where your staff may have answers on how to turn that negative into a positive. If you don't communicate daily, your staff will fill in the blanks with what they believe or perceive is happening in the company and being human nature it typically won't be positive. As a leader you must be open and honest just as Jack Welch stated, "Tell people the truth, because they know the truth anyway."[36]

Being accessible is important for good communication between you and your staff. I'm sure everyone reading this currently has or can remember a leader that they had who hid away in their office. No one liked to approach them or talk to them. This type of leader destroys positive communication and thus the respect of their staff. A good leader needs to be approachable at all times. Not to say that you must become everyone's personal psychologist because you will need to draw a line or people will take advantage of your accessibility and production will be hindered. You will need to be available to discuss all work related issues and as a part of connecting with your staff, listening to their personal life at times. Stop what you are working on, make eye contact and give them your full attention. An important point here is that you must be sincere about listening to your staff because they will know if you truly care about them by your demeanor. Connecting with others means you are not self-centered; that you focus on others because again, to communicate effectively you must listen first! Then you will know and understand how to speak to an individual in a way that will have impact. It is easy to find the best leader that is accessible in your company because it is the person that staff from other departments are communicating with most frequently. Former GE CEO Jack Welch stated, "Above all else, good leaders are open. They go up, down and around their organizations to reach people. They don't stick to established channels. They're informal. They're straight with people. They make a religion out of being accessible.[37]"

    When you become accessible to your staff, you know there will be those who will want to talk to you about everything they see wrong. Every leadership position I've ever held, there has always been at least one person that fits this scenario and when I was a young leader I didn't know how to handle it properly. Time was wasted as I listened to "this being wrong" or "this needs to be done differently" and it only made me depressed at times and added more work to my day as I researched the issues to see if they were valid and how to remedy them. I found that there some staff that complained just to complain and their perceived issues held no validity and didn't need to be addressed. I finally came up with a plan which I communicated with the staff. I had no problem listening to any perceived problems and issues but I wouldn't listen to them unless the staff bringing it to my attention also had a potential solution. This eliminated those who complained about issues that really weren't but it also empowered the staff to help to find solutions since they were the ones directly being affected by the issue. It didn't mean I would always accept and implement every idea but when I did and gave them credit for the solution, it showed that the staff was valued and communication, production and respect increased. "Nothing lifts a person, like being respected and valued by others." ~John C. Maxwell[38]

Communication has no impact if it is not credible and not being credible can erode any respect that you have earned. How often do you hear a child ask their parent to be able to do something and the parent blindly responds with a yes and sometimes with yes I promise? It drove my son nuts at first because he would ask if we could go somewhere and my response was always I can't promise it. People are so attuned to hearing either a yes or no and kids will take that yes or no literally as a promise. I always explained that I would never promise to do something just to make him happy at the moment if there was ever a chance that it may not happen later. Why? Because then I would lose credibility with everything and anything I told him. The same holds true with your staff. As a leader your word means everything and if you can't back it up with actions, which are more important, then you will have no credibility or respect from your staff. My staff always knew that if I said that I would find out an answer for them or would go to bat for them, that I would actually fulfill my word. They might not always like the result or answer I would get but my staff knew that I heard their concerns, wishes and hopes and valued them.

Credible communication is also believing whole heartedly in the message you are delivering to your staff. You have to believe what you are saying! You tell your staff that your department is going to exceed expectations for the month, you must believe it yourself because if you don't believe it then your staff sure isn't going to believe it. And don't think you can fake it, because your staff as you probably will admit are smart enough to pick up on any nuances in your speech or body movements that indicate your doubt. The corporate world could learn this lesson from the military. In World War II on June 6 1944, 150,000 troops stormed the beaches of Normandy, France which is now called D-Day. They were tasked with taking the German forces that were dug in, established, held the advantage of the high ground and even knew an attack was imminent, a task that any military planner will tell you held a low percentage of success on paper. But, every one of those 150,000 troops expected success and a victory and why? The leaders, some of our best in history such as Gen Dwight Eisenhower, who relayed the plans and orders believed in the success of the mission and this belief filtered throughout the troops. In a life or death scenario, if military leaders can relay a credible communication of belief that something can be accomplished with success, what prevents you from believing in your message to your staff.

    A strong leader must establish a relationship with their staff then they will be able to communicate effectively with them. It is hard to make either one of these more important than the other because they go hand in hand in connecting with your staff. And if you don't connect with your staff, you won't be able to in other aspects of leadership; gain your staff's respect, get them to perform their responsibilities because they want to, have any credibility or be able to move up through the leadership chain and advance your career. These two aspects can be some of the toughest things to learn and master but be sure when you do that you are not mimicking someone else's style but that it is your own. You will not find long term success being someone else. As a young leader, find your own style through learning, observing, experience and experimentation. President Gerald Ford understood the importance of learning good communication early when he said, "If I went back to college again. I'd concentrate on two areas; learning to write and to speak before an audience. Nothing in life is more important than the ability to communicate effectively."[39]

"The message emerging from a leader whom we trust is said to be a leadership message. Such a message is rooted in the character of the individual as well as his or her place within the organization. The leadership message is essential to the health of the organization because it stems from one of the core leadership behaviors – communication. Of all the leadership behaviors, the ability to communicate may be the most important. Communication lays the foundation for leading others."[40] Use great communication to ignite excitement which in turns will increase work production and cause your staff to move into a state of action instead of going through the day with their only goal to leave and go home.

RESPECT AS A LEADER

An aspect of human nature states that we do not like to give up control of situations to others where that situation could negatively affect us. Take a look at the workforce in 2018 compared to 30 years ago. In 2001, 80% of the workforce was now made up of knowledge / white collar workers and I'm sure that number will continue to increase. "At best leaders have an illusion of control of this workforce. You cannot command commitment from highly skilled employees. They reserve the right to decide how active and committed they are."[41]

The question arises then, is it possible to lead in the 21st century when corporate America still wants to operate as always, when employee relation dynamics have changed. The answer is yes! But it requires one to embrace change, be willing to learn about oneself and your staff and change your perception of power and leadership. These are not new concepts or ideas, but in fact have been utilized by great leaders.

Let's try a short homework assignment. Write down the names of those who you think through history were great leaders and the successful company, organization or nation they led. Now write down names of companies that haven't been successful or have had struggles and who led the company. I bet it was easy to remember the name of the leaders of successful companies but you couldn't remember as easily, if at all, the names of those who led troubled companies. What is the common thread of the successful leaders? The answer would be how they viewed and led their staff. "History teaches us that when controlling or authoritative managers leave, their control is greatly diminished; but when influential leaders leave, their influence remains, often indefinitely."[42] Do you want your legacy to quickly diminish or for people to remember your contributions for years to come.

Walt Disney stated, "Leadership means that a group, large or small, is willing to entrust authority to a person who has shown judgment, wisdom, personal appeal, and proven competence."[43] You need the ability to win minds in order to be successful. Dwight D Eisenhower remarked, "Now I think, speaking roughly, by leadership we mean the art of getting someone else to do something that you want done because he wants to do it, not because our position of power can compel him to do it, or your position of power." These two great leaders understood how and what it took to lead any group of individuals. They set aside their ego and power which they could have wielded authoritatively, but chose instead to lead with respect to their staff.

You have now mastered or at least are working on your relationship skills with your team and to build on that, you need to learn how to respect your staff. In order to receive respect from your staff, you must be able to give respect sincerely and continually. Your staff can and will know if the respect is sincere. Examples of respect are acknowledging accomplishments, giving credit where credit is due, treating staff fairly, checking your ego at the door or better yet eliminate your ego, protecting staff from the politics of the company, making them apart of the decision process and ideas and relinquish responsibilities to them, just to name a few.

As mentioned earlier, workers over the past years feel as they were only a cog in the wheel of the business machine where only a few benefit from the success of the company. The tables are turning as knowledge workers are increasing at a rapid rate and have the ability to determine how productive a company is.

Herb Kellecher, Former CEO and founder of Southwest Airlines states, "You have to treat you employees like customers. When you treat them right, then they will treat your outside customers right. That has been a powerful competitive weapon for us. You've got to take the time to listen to people's ideas. If you just tell somebody no, that's an act of power and, in my opinion an abuse of power. You don't want to constrain people in their thinking."[44]

    To give full respect though, you will have to take chances such as giving your staff the ability to make decisions and come up with new ideas. This can be scary to a new leader because they will feel as though their personal actions are being closely watched and any decision good or bad will affect them personally. Remember though that leadership is not a solo act but requires the action of bringing others along with you. If you maintain the thinking that you have to accomplish everything by yourself, then you are not respecting your staff and acknowledging their talents and abilities. Remember the saying two heads are better than one. Trying to go solo will ultimately have a negative impact on your ability to lead and in other areas of your life as well. I had a job where there was a manager in his twenties who thought he would be able to retire by age 40. He would make all decisions on his own, work longer hours than he really needed to, had no social life even though he was married and was constantly stressed. Retiring by age 40 may be a great goal to have except due to all the stress and trying to do everything himself, he physically looked over 40 and was sick and worn down all the time even though he was only in his twenties. Imagine if he respected the staff around him and utilized their skills and talents. He would have gotten the same if not more work accomplished with less stress, would have had a better standard of life and could maintain the goal of retiring early.

A great example of a leader who was not afraid to rely on others was General George Marshall whom, after Pearl Harbor, called Ike to his office and told him to draft a plan to save the Philippines. Ike took a few hours, then reported that it was not possible but suggested alternatives. Marshall said, "Eisenhower, the department is filled with able men who analyze their problems well but feel compelled always to bring them to me for final solution. I must have assistants who will solve their own problems and tell me later what they have done." To General Marshall, leadership was not about pleasing the boss or saying the right words; leadership was doing the right thing. This was the creed by which he lived.[45]

Taking credit for your staff's accomplishments or ideas has been a leadership disease throughout time. A quick way to loose respect from your staff is to tell your superior that you solely were responsible for the success of a project or idea and on the flip side blaming your staff for any problems or failures. Your superior typically didn't get to where they are by being a weak leader and most likely will recognize your deception eventually so it won't benefit you anyway to take sole credit for your staff's success. A strong leader is humble and has no problem publicly recognizing the accomplishments of his staff. Your staff will respect you for it and in return are more willing to perform at a higher level because they want to.

Another example of respect is not abusing perceived power. When I served in the US Army we had officers that were in their particular position only due to the rank they held. Some of these officers falsely believed that because of their rank they had power and were deserved of respect. The saying we had for these officers was that we saluted them only because of their rank as per military custom but we weren't saluting them as a person. An example of this was when I was in an Intelligence Unit stationed in a highly secure building and we were just beginning to get computers which were meant for secure work and I was responsible for the security of these computers. I had a Captain one day decide that he would type a personal document on the computer and I approached him about the improper use. He threatened to write me up for insubordination and he could do whatever he wanted on that computer until I mentioned that he should be willing to tell a superior officer who was ultimately in charge of the computer the same thing. Most officers though understood that rank didn't mean respect and power but the respect had to be earned.

Respect acknowledges the human aspect of leadership. Your staff are human with all the good and bad aspects that go with it but one thing that every human wants in life is to be respected and feel valued. Good leaders are able to and willing to work with and through the good and bad of human nature. Past decades home and work life were separated pretty definitively by the time clock and while at work, leadership were only concerned about one thing, production from the staff at any cost. In the 21st century home and work life are becoming more and more overlapped and knowledge workers are demanding respect. Carly Fiorina, former CEO of HP, wrote, "Human potential is the one limitless resource we have and yet it is wasted every day. In our world and throughout our communities and places of work and workshop, we face both vast opportunities and enormous difficulties. We can confront these only through creativity, leadership, empathy, determination, collaboration and problem-solving. We can only master challenges by unlocking human potential."[46] HP was struggling and was able to grow under Carly's direction. She understood that her employees needed to be valued and respected because they had the limitless potential to achieve anything including solve the company's problems if they were free to be a part of the solution.

    As a leader you will never be perfect, you are only human. How does this affect the respect you have earned from your staff? That all depends on how you handle the situation. Most leaders will inherently believe that they can't show any weakness or make mistakes because their staff will either lose respect for them or take advantage of the weakness. The opposite is actually true though. The more human you allow yourself to be perceived as, the more your staff will be able to connect and relate to you. The respect level increases as well because your staff will see that you don't allow your ego to control your actions. Author and pastor Rick Warren writes, "The most essential quality of leadership is not perfection but credibility. People must be able to trust you."[47] Leaders need to put aside the fear of appearing human, without faults and not knowing everything. History has given us many leaders who were respected and considered credible even though they weren't perfect and stumbled as human beings. The key is admitting your mistakes and your shortcomings. You will garner respect from everyone including your staff when you do this.

Besides making mistakes as a leader there is the fact that you can't know everything. Admit what you don't know. It is impossible for someone to know everything. Humility can go a long way by admitting to a subordinate that they know more about something than you do. And that is the way it should be. Rudy Giuliani states, "One of the most important qualities of leadership is being humble and understanding your limitations."[48] As mentioned I've heard Rudy Giuliani speak several times and one of the things he talks about and something I've tried to practice is hiring staff that are smarter than you in areas that you lack. You are to be the leader guiding the large overview of the mission while your staff specialize in specific tasks that need to be accomplished. Remember we are moving away from the idea that a leader needs to do everything themselves. "No one accomplishes anything of significance without the help of others. Leaders, in particular need the support of many people to achieve their business, professional, and personal goals."[49] You are still ultimately still personally responsible for the outcome of the mission but it will become easier when your staff knows they are trusted and can use their talents fully. The sense of accomplishment is greater for employees in the knowledge based workforce when they are able to see a positive outcome that they were personally involved with. I had a CEO once that created a program for advertising our product and I was responsible for ensuring the programs was implemented and performed. After a month, I realized that we were spending a lot of money for no results and approached him with the facts. He was a leader who thought he knew everything and what was best. A few more months went by and we had another meeting about the program where he said everyone including his accountant said the program was not viable and costing too much money for no positive results. He held his ground because it was his program and that meant it was a good program. Sadly, to say along with this program and the lack of humility to accept he didn't know everything, the company went out of business. If he had humbled himself and listened to those he placed in positions to advice, he might still be in business.

As a leader of a knowledge based staff in the 21st century, be humble, admit you don't know everything, hire people smarter than you that can fill in your shortcomings and trust them to do what you hired them to do.

COACHING AS A LEADER

A strong leader hires those smarter than themselves and gets out of the way and trust their staff to get the job done. But, you are still responsible for the outcome and shortcomings which strikes fear in leaders and paralyzes and prevents them from growing as leaders. Fear of your staff not performing does not have to be a part of the equation for a leader. You have the ability to control the work production of your staff by creating good relationships, positive communication and ensuring your staff is trained.

Your staff needs to be competent in their duties if you are going to be able to let them perform their duties to their fullest ability and not micro-manage them. Training budgets are being slashed from many companies but staff still need to keep up to date in their fields. The world is moving and changing at a rapid rate no matter the job title so the leader needs to adapt to this as well. Capt. Marquet in his book realized that learning is better than training.[50] Training is equated to passivity where something is done to us like a teacher standing at the front of a class telling how to perform an action while learning is active and requires someone to perform an action. When serving in the U.S. Army, I had an Imagery Analyst who was a subordinate and he was constantly making mistakes. I wouldn't show him where he was missing things he should have seen but would make him go back and re-examine the film. If I had shown him, he would have been a passive learner but by making him take action, he became active in his own learning. He complained about how I was working with him but he went on to be one of my best Imagery Analysts and would thank me later for direction. If you constantly tell your staff how to do their job then they have no reason to learn their craft. In addition, if your staff needs to be constantly told what to do then they really don't know how to do their job and you have a bigger problem.

As a leader you are going to need to institute a system where your staff not only have time to learn but are actively practicing their job functions. I am guilty of this many times, a task arises that I have performed before but don't remember how to perform it since I haven't done it in a while. In addition there may be new and better ways to perform the task which I haven't kept up with. Everyone including yourself must continue to learn and look to the future because new ideas, insights and approaches will help your team stay ahead of the competition. A competent staff goes beyond just being able to do their job properly at all times. It allows a leader to delegate more decision making which in turn results in a greater engagement and initiative and then ultimately higher employee productivity and morale. With a higher employee engagement, they begin to take the initiative to learn on their own without direction.

    A competent staff that is engaged in the advancement of the team and company is a litmus test of a good leader. Things can get done because your staff wants to accomplish the mission without you having to strong arm them to do so. Your staff become self-motivated, self-confident and get results. Team work and collaboration increases because everyone begins to respect and trust each other more knowing that everyone is looking out for each other and not just themselves. A great example of this is a phenomenon that occurred during the Iraq and Afghanistan wars. Soldiers were being shot and having body parts blown off but there was story after story of those who after going through therapy, went back to war. Most people can't comprehend why someone would do that but when asked why they wanted to go back, they always said, "That is my team over there and we look out for each other." Can you imagine if every department and every company had teams that felt and acted this way. Think about what could be accomplished if everyone was outward focused versus self-centered. Your competition wouldn't stand a chance and if you look at the most successful companies you will be able to see these actions every time. "It doesn't matter how brilliant a plan is if your team can not execute it."[51] As the leader, this is your goal which you have to demonstrate by your actions. Walt Disney probably said it best, "Whatever we accomplish belongs to our entire group, a tribute to our combined effort."

The more your staff works like a team and becomes engaged in producing at their highest levels, the more you will be able to set your staff free to utilize their talents. This not the same as empowering your staff to perform their job. Empowering is an oxymoron when you tell your staff, "You can make a decision if needed but do what you were told.

Empowering is essentially a form of manipulation by allowing someone to think they are an active participant but in reality they are only doing what they are told.[52] In many of my leadership positions, I tell my staff that they can make decisions as needed to get the mission accomplished particularly when I wasn't around. This can be a scary thing since I would ultimately be held responsible for anything that goes wrong but I want my staff to know that I trust them to be engaged, use their talents and expertise to resolve problems and make the company better. I would then give credit to them for positive actions but would except blame when something went wrong. The key is knowing your staff is trained well enough to make the right decision when needed.

    A leader shouldn't want a staff that only blindly go about their day doing their work, but instead consciously performs every task for the betterment of the company and questions something if a particular action would be detrimental. Even your best staff member will become discouraged and work as a zombie if their ideas and innovations are not recognized, it is only human nature. Encourage your staff to debate among themselves and with you about the direction of the mission. Healthy debate with diverse opinions will only strengthen the team and build positive commitment to the company. A company is going to grow when their staff are committed to the mission and when they are that way because they want to be. Whenever someone is put in a positive culture and environment they will inherently succeed.

"My passion has been to build an enduring company where people were motivated to make great products. Everything else was secondary." ~ Steve Jobs[53] Apple is an example of a company succeeding in the 21st century even while others are struggling. Steve Jobs understood that profits were only possible if Apple's employees were motivated and challenged to succeed.

"He infused Apple employees with an abiding passion to create groundbreaking products and a belief that they could accomplish what seemed impossible."[54] Every great leader has understood this concept, that money and profits are not the primary indicators and path to business success. Good leaders entrust their staff and challenge the process but the leader maintains an eye on the details which is what Steve Jobs did. Colin Powell, former Chairman of the Joint Chiefs of Staff and retired four star General, wrote "But as companies get bigger, they often forget who "brought them to the dance."[55]

    Companies and their leadership are afraid of the stockholders, afraid the economic environment, afraid of the customer and afraid of their employees. What companies have forgotten, as mentioned by Colin Powell, is that its employees have taken them to where they are and are capable of resolving stockholder, economic environment and customer fears.

Currently there is a flock of leaders that are afraid that they are going to lose their job if they don't do everything themselves. They feel that the saying, "If something is going to be done right, I have to do it myself," is the way to conduct business because they are not going to allow someone else be the reason they are demoted or fired. What corporate America doesn't realize is that this style of leadership is actually costing companies billions of dollars and future growth. General Patton stated, "90% of being in command is ensuring orders are followed. Give them, get out of the way and let people do their job."[56]

    A leader who just wants their staff to follow their orders without question can be referred as autocratic, command & control, coercion and the dreaded micro-manager. In *Turn the Ship Around!,* Captain Marguet states that with this type of leadership style, people are resigned to working as drones because suggestions are ignored, creativity and innovations under-appreciated and people stop trying.[57] Employees no longer feel connected to the company nor care about the success of it. They spend more time complaining about their leaders, the direction of the company, taking breaks, surfing the internet and working at the slowest pace possible just to get through their work day. In the 21st century, awards, bonuses and paychecks are no longer enough to keep the workforce motivated. People are looking to be recognized and appreciated for what they can offer the company and to be able to use their talents to the best of their ability. Stephen R Covey wrote, "You may be able to "buy" a person's back with a paycheck, position, power or fear, but a human being's genius, passion, loyalty, and tenacious creativity are volunteered only."[58]

    The United States has a strong legacy of having a strong workforce but over the past few decades it seems as though business has forgotten about the contributions of the workforce.

Obstacles have been put in place internally in companies that prevent staff to share their talents and knowledge for the betterment of the company. We all complain about how bureaucratic governments are but business is just as much so. Jack Welch says, "The way to get faster, more productive, and more competitive is to unleash the energy and intelligence and raw, or self-confidence of the American worker, who is still by far the most productive and innovative in the world. The way to harness the power of these people is not to protect them, not to sit on them, but to turn them loose, let them go, and get the management layers off their backs, the bureaucratic shackles off their feet, and the functional barriers out their way."[59]

    You must be competent as well at your position and know how to perform your staff's jobs even if you aren't as good at it as they are. Granted there will be specialized positions that as a leader you won't be able to accomplish but you should at least have an understanding of what the position requires, how the job needs to be performed and what the final outcome should be. As a leader you must be demonstrating your best every day because your staff isn't going to follow someone who can't follow through with their talk. I've always told my staff that I will jump off a bridge with them but if I don't back that up by getting my hands dirty then my credibility with my staff becomes suspect. General Colin Powell stated, "You can issue all the memos and give all the motivational speeches you want, but if the rest of the people in your organization don't see you putting forth your very best effort every single day, they won't either."

Being a leader, you must be out front leading the charge and being a problem solver when situations arise. Your employees are not going to follow through with getting the mission accomplished at their highest abilities unless they see you doing it firsthand. You have to be optimistic and know that there is a solution to every road block. I worked for a company where one of our mottos was, "We don't know how we are going to get it done but we will figure it out and get it done." In order to be a leader you must have problem solving skills, because you are requiring your employees to do the same thing. When your employees see your optimism in solving problems they will inherit that optimism and find it easier and easier to think on their feet and productivity will increase exorbitantly.

Employees of the 21st century perform better and are more productive with the actions I have described so far, but they are still human and have been programmed by our culture to just take orders and do as told. You will still have those who are reluctant to embrace change and no matter how competent your staff is they will still make mistakes. Under previous leadership styles, work environments and even human nature, people will try to hide and even avoid admittance to making mistakes. Mistakes meant write-ups and as many employee manuals probably state, "up to and including termination." But your staff has to understand that in order for them to have an active involvement in the company, they must also be willing to accept ownership for any mistakes. And as a leader you need to create a culture where mistakes are acceptable. I'm not talking about someone that makes the same mistake over and over again, this individual would qualify for retraining, discipline action or even termination. The mistakes I'm discussing are from someone taking the initiative to get something done or unintentionally making a mistake.

I was a manager at a newspaper which had 24 hour operations and was on-call when I wasn't there. Each of my staff for the most part worked at the newspaper in one function or another for over 15 years each. Combined they were so competent they knew every aspect of putting out a newspaper but unexpected problems still arose at various times that required a decision to be made immediately in order to get the paper out. I gave them control to make those decisions and just inform me the next day. They knew that if they did make a mistake that they didn't have to be afraid to tell me and that I would handle it with my superior. By leading like this, a 20 year veteran of the paper told me I was the best manager he had ever had. Even on a nuclear submarine, Capt. Marquet, realized that focusing solely on avoiding mistakes was a debilitating approach to the operation. I am in full agreement of his idea that focusing on avoiding mistakes takes focus away from striving for excellence.[60]

    Excellent leaders prepare for the time that they are given the opportunity to move up the corporate ladder. I'm not talking about preparing yourself but preparing your employees. You have done a disservice to your employees and company if you have not prepared people within your department of filling your position.

Rudy Giuliani is, "convinced that leadership is something we don't spend enough time teaching to people."[61] I have heard many times, which I agree with, a person is not ready or deserve to be promoted if they have not prepared their department to be able to continue to operate productively as though nothing happened. Picking the employee that is the constant "yes man" to be your replacement is the worst thing you can do. It can't be discussed enough in this book that everyone is their own person and everyone needs to be treated as a human. A "yes man" is essentially a drone robot who is incapable of thinking for themselves. Former executive at Xerox Barry Rand stated, "…if you have a yes-man working for you, one of you is redundant." As a leader you should be coaching all of your employees how to be effective future leaders and allowing them to grow according to their personality. The right person will blossom and it will become evident when the time comes who should be your replacement or promoted to a higher position. Marissa Mayer calls it, "Fluid leadership – the notion that everyone is equipped to do another's job and anyone could step in and succeed."[62] The top companies make leadership training a priority during good and bad times. John Larrere head of Hay Group an international a human resources consulting firm states, "The best companies for developing leaders recognize the value of strong leadership in both the good times and the bad. Culturally they just cannot do away with leadership development, even in recession. They don't see it as a perk but as a necessity."[63] Of the best companies for leaders, 94% actively manage a selection of successors for critical roles.

But, how do staff and those in leadership learn how to be leaders. Primarily it is through observation. Just like a kid growing up, they learn their good and bad behaviors from their parents, adults, and world around them. The same holds true unfortunately for leaders in corporate America. Very few companies have training programs to ensure new and seasoned leaders continue to learn leadership techniques. Many of the ones that do have leadership training are only doing it sporadically and are only going through the motions so that they can say they have a program. Companies that want to succeed in the future need to reassess their viewpoint on leadership training.

    Studies show that executives learn leadership through 20% bosses, coaches and mentors and 10% through formal courses and books.[64] This leaves 70% to learn from the sink or swim method. The top 20 companies for leadership development showed 100% had active CEOs in developing leadership talent compared to 65% of other companies outside of the top 25.[65] "Organizations with the highest quality leaders were 13 times more likely to outperform their competition in key bottom-line metrics such as financial performance, quality of products and services, employee engagement, and customer satisfaction."[66] And finally, "People at the Best Companies for Leadership sense the urgency to develop leaders more than their industry peers. In fact, while 94% of respondents among the Best Companies for Leaders say their organization actively manages a pool of successors for mission-critical roles, only 68.6% of the other organizations surveyed report the same."[67]

    You need to start the process of training your staff for leadership by giving your staff the opportunity to make decisions and take action. Capt. Marquet offers the following phrases that he implemented with his crew. Phrases such as; "I intend to", "I plan on", "I will", and "We will" with an explanation of how they plan to act, gives staff the ability to think on the next level.[68]

VALUES OF A LEADER

Mistakes and errors are going to occur but how they are handled dictates how involved your staff will be. Human nature states that we all are going to make mistakes no matter how competent or prepared we are. As the leader you should not be afraid to make mistakes. If you let fear immobilize you, then you are not going to accomplish anything. Lead by example or get out of the way, either lead or don't because there is no middle ground. If you make a mistake, own up to it, just make sure you act and keep moving forward. With the recent downturn of the economy, it is strong leaders that will be confident and courageous to step forward and take the lead. A strong leader will always be looking forward to the future and the path needed to get there. General Patton wrote, "Lack of orders is no excuse for inaction."[69] I worked for a family owned company where the CEO and owner was disconnected from the business. The employees would constantly state that the company ran despite the owner. As leaders in the company we didn't wait around for direction but did what we thought was best for the survival of the company. There is also the saying, "Just do it and ask for forgiveness later." There are obviously situations where this won't work but don't get stuck with the mentality, "If I haven't explicitly been told 'yes,' I can't do it." Good leaders believe, "If I haven't explicitly been told 'no,' I can."[70]

  Embrace the reality of situations head-on so that you can lead your staff in the right direction. Companies that have embraced the idea of giving their employees the authority to try new ideas without the fear of repercussion from mistakes are the ones that are innovating, growing and being profitable. Everyone who has had blackboards in their classrooms and heard fingernails run across it know how awful a sound that is. I always tell everyone I work with that my fingers on a chalkboard is when I hear someone say, "We have always done it that way," and the saying "If it isn't broke don't fix it," is an equivalent. Both of these sayings demonstrate a fear and complacency to act. Lee Cockerell, in his book *Creating Magic* states that saying we have always done it that way means it has been done wrong all along. If the past decade has taught us anything, is that everything is constantly changing, and is unpredictable. The companies that have been unwilling to adapt are no longer around or struggling to stay afloat. Jeff Bezos, CEO of Amazon wrote, "It's not that rare to hear a junior leader defend a bad outcome with something like, "We, we followed the process."[71] A more experienced leader will use it as an opportunity to investigate and improve the process." A good leader will not be afraid to try new things or methods of accomplishing the mission for their employees and company. You should always be looking at what is new in your industry and what is coming after that. The best way I've seen written to get this idea across came from General Powell, "Effective leaders create a climate where people's worth is determined by their willingness to learn new skills and grab new responsibilities, thus perpetually reinventing their jobs. The most important question in performance evaluation becomes not, "How well did you perform your job since the last time we met?" but, "How much did you change it?"[72]

Many established businesses and HR departments are going to fight you concerning your leadership style. There is historical and current proof that what is written in this book works but it doesn't match up with what is being taught in colleges or what they have been accustomed to. Change is a debilitating fear because as humans we inherently are afraid of the unknown. Don't be afraid though to pioneer the way of leading in a new and more effective manner. Your company will have no choice but to acknowledge your leadership style works when they witness your staff being the most productive team. The question then is how are you going to get your staff to buy into your leadership style? Building a relationship with positive communication, giving respect, leading by example, admitting that you make mistakes and being loyal to your staff. Jack Welch was a very successful CEO and he stated, "One of the things, about leadership is that you cannot be a moderate, balanced, thoughtful, careful articular of policy. You've got to be on the lunatic fringe."[73] Don't be afraid to lead the way to success.

    You are not going to get everyone to like you or be happy with you and attempting to do so is a sign of a weak manager. Have courage to state your opinions to your superiors and the leadership team with respect of course because you may have thought of something that no one may have that will enhance the company and mission at hand. Don't be afraid to confront your employees when needed to get the mission back on track or give guidance and direction. Lee Cockerell wrote, "A leader's job is to do what has to be done, in the way it should be done, whether you like it or not, and whether they like it or not."[74]

    Everyone can't be treated the same because each person is a different human being with their own unique personalities, past experiences and goals. Attempting to treat everyone the same will only tick off your most productive and effective employees. And keeping toxic employees in an environment that you are making positive is a recipe for disaster. As a leader you need to work with the toxic employee first and attempt to guide them to seeing the need to be positive and supportive of the mission because remember most people have been exposed to working in a negative environment but if they refuse to change their ways, don't be afraid to cut ties or reassign the employee.

General Patton wrote, "One of the most frequently noted characteristics of great men who have remained great is loyalty to their staff."[75] All of these changes are great but if your staff doesn't believe that you truly care for them then you will accomplish none of it. Take interest in your employee's non-work life and be sincere about it. And don't think you can fake it, because they will sniff it out if you are being fake. As humans we have adapted to not initially trust someone who claims to care about us. Most everyone's initial reaction towards someone attempting to reach out to us is, what does this person want from me or they just want to use me to accomplish something for them. When Yahoo CEO Marissa Meyer took over the first thing she did was to talk to the employees and get their ideas and feedback. And what she found out was they wanted a leader because they already knew what they needed to do, they just needed someone to tell them to go do it, get out of the way and run defense for them.[76]

As a leader attempting to change the dynamic of the corporate American culture, you are going to have to walk the walk and show proof before you will gain full loyalty from everyone on your staff. Bob Chapman, CEO of Barry-Wehmiller states, "No one wakes up in the morning to go to work with the hope that someone will manage us. We wake up in the morning and to work with the hope that someone will lead us."[77] One of the examples I used earlier about when I worked for the newspaper applies here. My staff were loyal to me for several reasons, I kept them informed about what was happening in the company, they had the ability to use their talents and intellect to get the job done, feedback was welcomed for improving job functions and that I would insulate them from my superiors if they made an unintentional mistake or because they took the initiative to get the paper out on time. Ask any current service member or veteran why they would put themselves at risk of injury or even death and the answer will always be "Because they would have done it for me?" Don't get me wrong though, protecting your staff from consequences for their negative continued behavior is irresponsible to the employee, yourself and the company. Calm correction goes along way compared to angry berating and the employee will know you are looking out for their best interest thus increasing trust and loyalty.

    Companies that have the greatest amount of success exhibit this quality. There are enough external negatives bombarding a company on a daily basis, competition, economic variables, publicity, customers, and many more. These external negatives can't be controlled for the most part but what happens internally within a company can be. Loyalty is a critical thread that needs to be woven throughout the whole organization. Too often competition among and within departments prevents loyalty from existing in a company. When employees are more focused on their own survival and protecting their job, the production of a company suffers. When a company is struggling from external and internal issues, the staff recognize it and will start to act for their own gain but when a company is strong, staff's actions will be based on the benefit of the company and each other. Excellent leaders need to prevent internal strife from preventing a productive culture of cooperation. You need to instill pride in the company. Companies, "…that out maneuver and out innovate their competitors, the ones that command the greatest respect from inside and outside their organizations, the one with the highest loyalty and lowest churn and the ability to weather every storm or challenge. The exceptional organizations all have cultures in which the leaders provide cover from above and the people in the group look out for each other."[78]

A part of being loyal is giving credit where credit is due. Staff have gotten accustomed to their superiors taking credit for their ideas and accomplishments. This scenario has stifled businesses as staff feel less inclined to produce knowing that they will not receive credit for their work. Good leaders put others in the center and themselves on the peripheral. Your staff will produce more and be highly innovative if they know that as a leader you will tell your superiors and others who rightly deserves the credit. Rewards and going away gifts can be a two edge sword though. People like to be recognized but there needs to be a system in place to ensure everyone is recognized appropriately. Your staff will recognize if you favor some people over others when it comes to recognition, which will make the recognition have no value and cause resentment within your team.

As a good leader, your staff should be producing and being productive because they want to and not for the potential award but proper recognition goes a long way. For some of your staff that is the motivational factor to continue to produce. It is customary in the military to give awards to those leaving a unit and after being stationed at my unit in Panama for almost 3 years, I was being given a medal. At the time I held the rank of Sergeant E-5 and had received other medal, for my actions while with the unit. On the same day a Warrant Officer was being given a medal before they left and they had been with the unit 6 months and had received no prior medals while with the unit. I was given a medal that ranked lower than my other medals I had received for my actions and the warrant officer was given a higher ranked medal. The justification by the commanding officer was that the warrant officer held a higher rank. This is an example where proper recognition was not given which caused the enlisted ranks in the room to question the loyalty of the commanding officer. I didn't need the medal to solidify everything I had accomplished and I felt proud of the mark I had left on the unit. I decided to refuse the medal and gave it back. It may have been the wrong thing to do even though it was not against Army policy but I felt that for others to be recognized properly in the future, I had to do it as a leader. "Research shows that the highest performing leaders are the most open and caring, the most positive and are more grateful than their lower performing counterparts."[79]

    With loyalty comes Integrity, something that is and has been lacking in business particularly over the past decade. Integrity is an essential part of being a great leader and your ability to get others to follow you. Employees trust in leaders falters when the leader takes credit for the success of their staff, says things to make themselves look better and avoid accountability for their mistakes. "To be a true leader, to engender deep trust and loyalty, starts with telling the truth."[80] This is true for any size company where a seamless little white lie might seem as though it might not hurt anyone. If your staff doesn't trust you, they will not follow you. That is why politicians are so despised as a whole anymore. Every election period, politicians publicly promise anything that they perceive will get them elected, but as soon as they are elected, they throw their promises in the trash. Promises and integrity are sacrificed by leaders too often to advance their own personal gain. "Managerial skills give you credibility; unless you are organized, do what you say you are going to do, and keep your promises, you will not be considered a great leader."[81] These type of leaders have a negative impact on the organization and ultimately their own success. Employees are not going to follow a leader they can't trust, this can lead to the leader having to resort to a dictatorship style of leading and ultimately no matter what the case, employees are not going to be productive which affects the company. Another negative impact of this type of leader is that the employees will view having little or no integrity as part of the culture of the company and will follow the leader's poor example. Companies see a loss of office supplies for personal gain, extended lunch hours, poor customer treatment and non-productive actions such as surfing the internet because the staff emulate what they see leadership doing. By having integrity at all times, the staff will respect you and follow your example and customers will be impressed thus making the company more profitable.

It will be tough to have integrity if you don't have a belief structure which drives your actions and thoughts. You must trust what you are saying and have confidence in how you say it. This goes hand in hand with integrity. Staff need to be able to trust their leader but they also need to see that the leader believes in what they are trying to accomplish. Too often we see people in leadership positions who are leading their team down a particular path but the leader is wishy-washy in whether they believe in the direction they are going. You can't lead anyone if you don't know what direction you are going. No staff or team is going to follow a leader like that and productivity is going to be greatly diminished. President Ronald Reagan is considered a strong leader of the 1980's and he had a strong belief in that communism was evil. His undying belief in this made it very easy for everyone to support him. Reagan didn't form this belief because of popularity polls or it if was going to improve or reduce his ratings but because he believed it wholeheartedly. "This is a leader. That is how you define leadership."[82] Yahoo CEO Marissa Mayer also states, "Lead your team by making your vision clear and always orienting them in the right direction to achieve these goals."[83]

Take a look at the top listed companies to work for and what is one thing you find in common? I'm willing to bet most will answer this incorrectly because in America we have been conditioned to look at work as a necessary thing where we wake up every morning and grudgingly head to an office for 9 hours of our life. But the top companies to work for have people that like going to work because it is rewarding and it is also fun.

I have worked for several different types of companies where there is a common attitude among those which have had difficulty succeeding or even went under. Have you ever sat in the break room before work or at lunch and noticed the demeanor of everyone? Everyone for the most part are happy, laughing and over all positive but what happens the minute they have to clock in for work. Their demeanor changes to one of seriousness. Everyone appears to hate their job and drudge around looking as if they are miserable. This is very unproductive and it spills over to every aspect of the business. A quote from Sir Richard Branson CEO of Virgin, "Some 80% of your life is spent working. You want to have fun at home; why shouldn't you have fun at work?"[84] I mentioned earlier in the book where I had a District Manager that told me to drive around the block if I didn't have a smile on my face when I got to work because my employees would pick up on it and replicate it. How many of you gone into a retail store and walked out thinking, those employees don't like working there? On the other hand one of my favorite stores to shop in is Home Depot because everyone seems to enjoy working there and are quick to assist me with any questions. Which store do you think is going to have better sales and have repeat customers.

In one of my last retail management positions as Operations Manager I was in charge of handling lay-away which can be a stressful and thankless job. So, the first day that customers could pick up their lay-away for Christmas, I made it fun and had the staff laughing and the customers smiling and commenting on how it was the best lay-away pickup experience they have ever had. My store manager though reprimanded me for everyone having fun even though there were no lost layaways which was not the norm and the lines were kept to a minimum with happy customers. Your staff's demeanor can even be heard over the phone when they talk to customers or vendors. What causes this change in people from the time they are hanging in the break room and they punch in for work? It is because the company does not see its employees as human or family but instead as numbers in the bottom line. The United States is considered the biggest capitalist market but it is declining because it has lost track of the importance of treating its workforce as humans.

A recent 2013 Gallup Poll titled State of the American Workplace found that when bosses ignore their employees, 40% of them will disengage from concentrating on work but when bosses criticize regularly only 22% disengage.[85] This sounds like a bad statistic but what it demonstrates is that even if the boss gives poor recognition, it is a type of recognition, and employees will be more engaged. Imagine if a boss was truly concerned about their employees and was actively recognizing them as humans, how engaged they would be to accomplish the company goals and mission. Never overlook the importance of having face to face time with your employees. Don't be afraid to apologize for your mistakes, it sets a good example and lets staff know you are human. General Colin Powell wrote and it works for the civilian world as well, "The day soldiers stop bringing you their problems is the day you have stopped leading them. They have either lost confidence that you can help them or concluded that you do not care. Either case is a failure of leadership."[86] Great examples of companies that are succeeding and are at the cutting edge of innovation all have environments and cultures that people truly enjoy coming to work and are happy such as Google, Apple, Pixar and Disney. As a leader you need to build a culture where people act the same way on the clock as they do off. You need to be an example and be authentic to who you are. Embrace the way you are. I have Disney items on my desk and walls but I don't worry about what others think. The staff respects this because I'm being me and leading by example. In the 21st century it is counterproductive to force people to have a clean desk with no personality, people work better when they feel relaxed and can express themselves.

RELAX AS A LEADER

Leadership inherently creates stress in one's life and you are taking care of your staff but what are you doing to take care of yourself. Studies keep coming out stating that people feel guilty taking time off from work, aren't using all of their earned vacation and when they do take time off they are still connected to work through email on their cell phones and laptops. Electronics has made it too easy to stay connected to everything and everyone at all times, and it is only going to get worse. Staff and particularly leaders are afraid that if they do take time for themselves, the company will hold it against them and possibly replace them with the current environment of laying people off. The thought process is there is always someone out there that can replace you and do your job for less pay. The United States has become a society that doesn't stop and truly relax and unwind. Of all the economically developed countries in the world, the United States is the only one that does not by law require companies to offer vacation time to its employees. Humans weren't created to work 24 hours a day, 7 days a week though. God created the earth in six days and on the seventh he rested and commanded man to do as well. You have to unplug from the stressors of work and the world and relax. I mentioned earlier about an IT manager in his mid-twenties that thought if he didn't stay connected to the job all of the time, that things would fall apart and it would prevent him from moving up in the organization so he could meet his goal of retiring by age 40. By the time he turned 30, he was balding, looked drained and as if he was in his 40's. His health had been severely impacted and his quality of life was constantly deteriorating along with his marriage. Just take a look the picture of any President of the United States when they first take office compared to what they look like 4-8 years later if you want to see what the bodily effects of leadership are.

No job is worth destroying your marriage, family or health. You need to find a balance in your life between work and those who are a priority in your life including yourself. First thing is to take back control of your life and do a self-assessment. You need to do your job but you can't let it consume you and dictate who you are and stop blaming others for your predicaments. What is really important in your life? Society has gotten to the point where answering an email or keeping up to date on social media has become priority in people's lives. Technology advancements have created a bunch of noise, essentially covering up a person's true priorities, family and self. You need to nurture your close relationships. "Close relationships are not business acquaintances or people in your network. (Note the word work hiding there!)[87] Make time to go to your kid's ballgames, recitals, and events and be sure to take your spouse on a date night every week if possible, minimum two times a month. "A man should never neglect his family for business." ~ Walt Disney Build those relationships and never let them stagnant or die. Part of nourishing your relationship with those that matter is to do one of the toughest things in our current culture. Pull back on having to have everything. Things don't bring happiness and only distract one's attention away from your family. Those new purchases and toys, do they bring you lasting memories, or do they create lasting memories for the whole family. Will your kids remember that fishing trip you took them on or will they remember you hovered over your laptop doing spreadsheets and answering emails, or better yet playing Xbox all the time when not at work.

    Human nature sometimes blocks us from doing a true self-assessment or admitting when we are getting too stressed and reaching our breaking point. It happens to everyone no matter how much you practice or implement what you have read in this book. That is why, at whatever leadership level you are, an accountability partner is needed. This person needs to be a trusted peer or superior that knows you well and never a subordinate. Your accountability partner requires permission to let you know when they perceive that you are getting stressed, leading incorrectly or any other negative actions, without you getting mad or defensive. Society may say this shows weakness and it is not acceptable to show any weak links in oneself, particularly a leader. Everyone, including those in leadership roles though are human and we all have weaknesses. Strength though is what is actually demonstrated and your staff will respect a leader who is willing to admit they also put their pants on one leg at a time like everyone else. This system will strengthen teamwork and trust in the company because everyone will be working towards the same goal of taking care of each other.

Because of all the changes you implemented as a true leader, from this book, you should have no reason not to be able to unplug and relax. You can rest comfortably knowing that your staff is able to function and make decisions based on the direction you gave them. David Marquet wrote, "The vast majority of situations do not require immediate decisions."[88] The United States has been involved in active war for a decade where decisions could result in life or death situations but those in the military still took leave (vacation), even those in leadership including the President took vacation and the combat missions were still accomplished. And I'm sure the majority that read this book are not involved in life or death decisions. Plus, you are now setting an example for your staff and they need to know it is ok to unplug and relax as well. Your group will be healthier, more mentally and emotionally prepared to handle everything and anything that is presented to them. "Have fun in your command. Don't always run at a breakneck pace. Take leave when you've earned it: Spend time with your families. Corollary: surround yourself with people who take their work seriously, but not themselves, those who work hard and play hard."[89]

Stop taking yourself so seriously. They say laughter is the best medicine and smiling uses less muscles than frowning. Go out and do things that you might consider childish or did as a kid and don't worry about what others think because they won't know what they are missing. I personally am a big Disney fan for many reasons and one of them is that every time I drive onto Disney property all stressors seems to be lifted from my shoulders. I can act like a kid and have fun, and any adult that visits Disney often knows what I'm talking about. "Too many people grow up. That's the real trouble with the world, too many people grow up." ~ Walt Disney Some of the best financially and innovative companies currently have slides between floors, ping pong and pool tables, various games and peoples desks are decorated with what many would call childish toys and they don't employ kids but adults.

Finally, stay humble. Every person in your company is important from the janitorial staff to the CEO. People respect and follow a leader who remains humble and realizes they wouldn't be where they are without the rest of their team. Remember, your staff dictates your future success, not you.

THE NEW WORKFORCE

No book on modern leadership in the 21st century would be complete without covering the topic of Millennials. While there are different dates describing when millennials were born, generally it is considered between 1982 – 2004. By 2025, it is estimated that millennials will represent 75% of the workforce. This generation have been labeled as the most entitled, laziest and high maintenance of all generations to date. "They will be the most high maintenance workforce in history of the world, but they may also be the most high performing." Says Bruce Tulgan, consultant and author of *It's Okay to Manage Your Boss.*[90] They have been coddled by parents, teachers and coaches where everyone is rewarded equally and each is told they are special. While at the same time building relationships via social media and comparing themselves to whatever others post. Based on all this, employers have been led to believe millennials are and will be a nightmare to hire and lead.

It turns out millennials want from their employer in the 21st century everything that has been discussed in this book and what every employee of previous generations wanted. "Appreciation, recognition, encouragement: ARE. Together they make up a cost-free, fully sustainable fuel, one that builds self-confidence and self-esteem, boosts individual and team performance, and keeps an organization running cleanly and smoothly."[91] There may be some differences as there always is between generations but what it comes down to is a strong leader will build a strong team no matter who is a part of it.

Millennials want to experience personal benefit and growth. Communication is key but any good leader should already have good communication with their staff. Part of this communication is constant feedback and not just once a year reviews. As a leader, you should be doing this anyway with all of your staff. People crave feedback, mostly positive reinforcement but they also want to know how they are doing in order to improve. No one likes getting to their yearly review and finding negative comments when they didn't even know they weren't performing well. Remember millennials were used to constant feedback from their parents, teachers and coaches and most of the time it was only positive. This generation, believe or not is willing to receive feedback even if it is not positive. They just want feedback and communication with their leader on a consistent basis.

As a part of the communication, millennials want to know the big picture and feel a part of accomplishing it. This applies really to all staff as mentioned early, too often people like they are left in the dark like mushrooms and fed a bunch of crap. Every staff member is important to the team for accomplishment of the ultimate goal no matter if they have been there 1 week or 20 years. Fresh ideas are always good and millennials want to contribute and have their ideas heard. They seek out and enjoy challenges and their experience and ability to harness the power of technology will help a company fulfill its goals more efficiently and more quickly. Leaders who embrace the abilities of millennials will find themselves ahead of their competitors.

    Communication for millennials means collaboration with their fellow workers. They are the most diverse group to enter the workforce and they embrace it. Millennials have grown up being able to talk to anyone in real time face to face from anywhere in the world through technology They don't see anyone else's status in life being abnormal because they grew up with different types of households; a mom and dad, single parents, two parents of the same sex, multicultural households and individuals that are of every sexual persuasion. This is the norm for them and they embrace it. Millennials enjoy working together to solve a problem and believe everyone's input is important and valid.

As mentioned early in the book, people don't want to be managed, they want to be led and have a purpose. The difference with millennials is that they haven't always been led towards their purpose since everything was always done for them, so this may take some extra time to accomplish. Expect to spend extra time teaching and coaching millennials how to accomplish their job. The same leadership works with millennials as it does for everyone else. They want to be led and have a purpose. "Leadership is communicating to people their worth and potential so clearly that they are inspired to see it in themselves." ~ Stephen R. Covey Millennials have stated they want to be led but they also expect respect for their ideas and want to be challenged.

Leaders may have to coach millennials more when it comes to relationships and instant gratification. Millennials don't understand that the important things in life take time since they are so used to everything in the past being instantly available at their fingertips and their parents giving them whatever they want. They need a leader who will guide them so that they understand that job fulfillment, self-confidence, relationships and skill sets take time. A leader will share the big picture with them but they need to be prepared to know that they may not understand fully, or have the skills to make an immediate impact, in fact it may take a few months or even a year to fully come up to speed fully.

Millennials are the first generation to experience growth at a fast pace such as new phones every year, games systems updating often and apps updating on a weekly basis. These experiences have enabled them to have a strong entrepreneurial mind which means seeing new solutions to problems which is beneficial for any company. Along with being entrepreneurial minded, millennials are the most connected generation ever. They know that if they need an answer to anything, it is at their fingertips within seconds from a vast amount of sources such as internet searches with results from multiple sources, social media and texts. This can be a two-edged sword though, due to the fact they are so connected, their networking skills are better and if they feel they are not appreciated or respected, they have a lot of resources to find a new job quickly.

    The number one reason millennials leave their job, which on average is every 2 years is due to their boss. They are not afraid to change jobs because everything in their world has been temporary anyway with the fast pace of technology. "Millennials no longer work for you; they work with you." Sort of sound similar to what I have been discussing all along. This is the same for everyone else, people don't leave their job because of the company but because of their boss. But if a leader follows what has been written in this book, they will find it very easy to work with millennials and in return they will be a great asset to the company.

Millennials find work & life balance to be very important. Others generations have been pushing for a change in this area but millennials are forcing the issue. The need to work traditional 9 to 5 hours at an office no longer exists in a knowledge based workforce. Technology enables people to work from anywhere and still collaborate in real-time which millennials have grown up with. There has been a large increase in people working from home due to advancement in technology and leaders in the 21st century need to embrace it or risk losing their best staff to companies that do. An estimated 3 million people already work from home with that number expected to increase by 63% over the next 5 years. [92]

Everything that millennials are requesting from a leader is in reality everything a leader should already be doing. The corporate culture has fought against these changes and ideals, and continue to do so for various reasons; company history, outdated leadership courses and apparent cost savings. Leaders and companies that refuse to or drag their feet to change their leadership strategies are going to find out their ideas will cost them more in the long run. Their competitors that do change will have the best trained and loyal staff and will take command of the marketplace. Companies and leaders that fight to change their leadership culture will quickly find out over the next few years, as millennials take over the majority of the workforce, they will have no choice but to change if they want their position or company to continue to exist.

CONCLUSION

The direction a leader takes dictates the culture of the company. I was working as an operations manager for a retail company and was being groomed to take over my store. The district manager, believed in training competent current employees to fill leadership positions as they became available. He was the one that told me about not entering the store without a smile on my face. One day the district manager left the company and a new one took his place. This new district manager sat in my office across from me within days of taking over and told me not expect advancement anytime soon because he had friends he wanted to put into positions. The atmosphere of the store changed and I left the company. This company is no longer in business. This is just a small example of bad leadership that concerns themselves with the perks and power that come with a position.

An example on a larger scale comes from the recent banking crisis where CEO's were ultimately forced from their positions but still left with what is considered a golden parachute of millions of dollars in severance. The biggest example of this was Stanley O'Neal at Merrill Lynch who alienated everyone around him, the company's largest quarterly loss in its 93 year history of $2.3 billion, a $8.4 million dollar fine from the government and forced from his CEO position but not before receiving $161.5 million in severance. It is well documented how O'Neal dismantled the culture of where employees were treated as family at Merrill Lynch but instead instituted a culture of fear. David Komansky who followed O'Neal as CEO wrote, "He never understood the culture of Merrill and what the phrase (Mother Merrill) meant to its employees. It meant a firm that was different – a firm that cared about them, that they cared about, and that had a familial feel to it." In 2005 Merrill Lynch spent

$163,685 on corporate jet flights and $198,394 on chauffeured car for O'Neal while he was compensated $37 million. O'Neal felt that he was the only one capable of resolving issues and led through micro-managing and an iron fist. Komansky stated, "That ultimately contributed to his downfall. By the time the subprime thing happened, he had no one left who supported him. When you are abusive as he was, so many times, to so many people, over such a long time, eventually things catch up to you." On March 7, 2008 at the House of Representatives Oversight and Government Reform Committee, Henry Waxman the committee chairman said, "Our economy is suffering. Thousands are losing their jobs. And it seems like everyone is hurting except for the C.E.Os who had the most responsibility."

    Policies and leadership that is derived from those living in ivory towers, such as CEOs of recent, have had a huge negative impact on employees and the company's bottom lines.

Meanwhile successful companies that have a positive culture, succeeding beyond expectations and loyal employees have leadership who are getting paid much less such as Costco's CEO Jim Sinegal who made $650,000 in 2012.[93] Weak cultures create an environment where everyone is looking out for their own personal gain instead of working together for the betterment of all. In *Leaders Eat Last* it states, "If good people are asked to work in a bad culture, one in which leaders do not relinquish control, then the odds of something bad happening go up. People will be more concerned about following the rules out of fear of getting in trouble or losing their jobs then doing what needs to be done."[94] A radical leadership change has to occur in the 21st century compared to the past few decades. At GE they have their own jargon and one of those terms is "Bullet Train" which describes GE's approach to change, "You can increase the speed of the bullet train somewhat by making modifications, but if you want it to go a lot faster, you have to make radical changes to the design of the train and the system on which it runs." [95] Successful companies of the 21st century will understand the need for change but more importantly they will have to act to make those changes.

In a weak environment the leader loses sight of the fact that if they are only looking out for their own personal gain then their staff has the power, as discussed earlier, of making it tougher for them to succeed and move up the chain of leadership. The unfortunate thing is that today's corporate structure and environment tends to encourage and breed leaders that lose the human side of leadership. This in turn destroys the inherent human nature to trust, as leaders and staff no longer have respect or trust for each other. Bad cultures are the breeding grounds for bad leaders who negatively impact the company over the long term.

Any leader who does look out for others, particularly their staff, will be viewed as a threat in a bad leadership culture. Don't be afraid to take a stand and believe in your staff. It may seem easier to fall into the same leadership style of those around you and human nature will drag you in that direction but stay strong and be a beacon of change. Lee Cockerell writes, "Because people naturally resist change, great leaders orient their people not only to expect change but to welcome it." [96] Your staff will trust and respect you. They will become more productive and the company will have no choice but to take notice. Your positive leadership style will create a new culture within the organization while those who are negative leaders will be forced to either embrace the change or leave.

Lead from the front always and make sure your staff sees you as a leader, demonstrate you are a servant leader sacrificing for your staff, show your human side and remember to have fun.

Jack Welch said, "…Don't sit still. Anybody sitting still, you can guarantee they're going to get their legs knocked out from under them." 97

NOTES

1. " https://www.merriam-webster.com", accessed 22 April 2014
2. "http://govleaders.org/quotes.htm", accessed 22 August 2014
3. " https://www.merriam-webster.com", accessed 22 April 2014
4. "https://eisenhower.archives.gov", accessed 14 July 2014
5. "http://www.think-energy.net/Colin-Powell-on-Leadership.pdf" *Leadership Primer*, accessed 18 January 2015
6. "https://ecorner.stanford.edu/video/the-difference-between-management-and-leadership", access 16 November 2014
7. "https://www.processexcellencenetwork.com/lean-six-sigma-business-transformation/columns/drucker-knew-that-leadership-had-incredible-power", accessed 2 January 14
8. Janet Lowe, *Jack Welch Speaks: Wisdom From The World's Greatest Business Leader* (New York: John Wiley & Sons Inc., 1998) 71.
9. Department of the Army Pamphlet 600-65: Leadership Statements and Quotes (Washington DC: Headquarters Department of the Army, 1985)
10. L. David Marquet, *Turn The Ship Around!: A True Story of Turning Followers Into Leaders* (New York: Penguin Group, 2015) 202.

11. Charles M. Province, *Tactical Leadership Skills for Business Managers: Patton's One-Minute Messages* (New York: Random House Publishing Group, 1995) p. 17.
12. Simon Sinek, (2014) *Leaders Eat Last: Why Some Teams Pull Together and Others Don't* [Kindle] Retrieved from http://amazon.com, 8-9.
13. Lee Cockerell, *Creating Magic: 10 Common Sense Leadership Strategies From a Life at Disney* (London: Vermilion, 2008) 31.
14. "http://theafle.org/recommended-reading" *Ten Leadership Truths*, accessed 2 January 2014
15. *Leaders Eat Last,* 9.
16. Bruce Klatt & Murray Hiebert, *The Encyclopedia of Leadership: A Practical Guide to Classic and Contemporary Leadership Theories and Techniques* (New York: McGraw-Hill Companies, 2000) 291.
17. "https://eisenhower.archives.gov", accessed 14 July 2014
18. Department of the Army Pamphlet 600-65
19. D. Michael Abrashoff, (2002) *It's Your Ship: Management Techniques From the Best Damn Ship in the Navy* [Kindle] Retrieved from http://amazon.com
20. *Leadership Primer*
21. *Tactical Leadership Skills for Business Managers,* 24.
22. "http://www.nytimes.com/2012/03/14/opinion/why-i-am-leaving-goldman-sachs.html" *Why I Am Leaving Goldman Sachs*, accessed 25 July 2014

23. John C. Maxwell, *5 Levels of Leadership: Proven Steps to Maximize Your Potential* (New York: Center Street Hachette Book Group, 2011) 68.
24. *The Quotable Walt Disney* (New York: Disney Press, 2001)
25. "https://www.ziglar.com/category/quotes/", accessed 13 February 2014.
26. Department of the Army Pamphlet 600-65
27. *5 Levels of Leadership,* 67.
28. *Creating Magic,* 27.
29. "https://inside.ucumberlands.edu/academics/history/downloads/MorningInAmericaVol4I1.pdf", *Principled Leadership in a Time of Crisis,* accessed 12 October 2014.
30. John Baldoni, (2003) *Great Communication Secrets of Great Leaders* [Kindle] Retrieved from http://amazon.com.
31. Judith Orloff, *The Top Performer's Guide to Leadership: Essential Skills That Put You On Top* (Naperville: Sourcebooks Inc., 2008) xii.
32. *Turn The Ship Around!,* 161.
33. John C. Maxwell, *Everyone Communicates, Few Connect: What the Most Effective People Do Differently* (Nashville: Thomas Nelson, 2010) 17.
34. *Turn The Ship Around!,* 74.
35. *Jack Welch Speaks,* 135.
36. *Jack Welch Speaks,* 35.
37. *Jack Welch Speaks,* 89.
38. *5 Levels of Leadership,* 113.
39. *Everyone Communicates, Few Connect,* 18.
40. *Great Communication Secrets of Great Leaders*

41. *The Encyclopedia of Leadership,* 274.
42. *The Encyclopedia of Leadership,* 275.
43. Bill Capodagli & Lynn Jackson, *The Disney Way: Harnessing the Management Secrets of Disney In Your Company* (New York: McGraw-Hill, 1999).
44. "http://archive.fortune.com/magazines/fortune/fortune_archive/2001/05/28/303852/index.htm", *The Chairman Of the Board Looks Back As Herb Kelleher hands over the controls, he tells FORTUNE's Katrina Brooker what it took to make Southwest Airlines a great--if wacky--company. How did he do it? His way.* accessed 18 July 2014
45. Ed Cray, *General of the Army: George C. Marshall, Soldier and Statesman* (New York: Cooper Square Press, 2000) 265-266.
46. "http://carlyfiorina.com/about" *About Carly.* accessed 3 January 2014
47. *5 Levels of Leadership*, 100.
48. "http://www.esquire.com/features/what-ive-learned/ESQ0503-MAY_RUDY#newsletter_righttrail" *What I've Learned: Rudy Giuliani.* accessed 13 December 2013
49. *The Encyclopedia of Leadership,* 294.
50. *Turn The Ship Around!,* 129.
51. *Turn The Ship Around!,* 42.
52. *Turn The Ship Around!,* 41.
53. "http://hbr.org/2012/04/the-real-leadership-lessons-of-steve-jobs/ar/pr" *The Real Leadership Lessons of Steve Jobs,* accessed 14 April 2012

54. "http://hbr.org/2012/04/the-real-leadership-lessons-of-steve-jobs/ar/pr" *The Real Leadership Lessons of Steve Jobs,* accessed 14 April 2012
55. *Leadership Primer*
56. *Tactical Leadership Skills for Business Managers,* 20.
57. *Turn The Ship Around!,* 174.
58. *Turn The Ship Around!,* 15.
59. *Jack Welch Speaks,* 121.
60. *Turn The Ship Around!,* 43.
61. *Principled Leadership in a Time of Crisis*
62. "http://blog.creativegroup.com/how-to-be-a-better-leader-marissa-mayer-dreamforce-2013", *How to Be a Better Leader: Marissa Mayer at Dreamforce 2013,* accessed 10 April 2014.
63. "http://www.businessweek.com/printer/articles/328206-how-companies-develop-great-leaders?type=old_article", *How Companies Develop Great Leaders,* accessed 25 July 2014.
64. "http://www.ccl.org/leadership/pdf/research/GroomingTopLeaders.pdf", *Grooming Top Leaders: Cultural Perspectives from China, India, Singapore and the United States* accessed 12 October 2014
65. ""http://www.inspireimagineinnovate.com/pdf/Top_Companies_2005_Report.pdf", *How the Top 20 Companies Grow Great Leaders,* accessed 10 October 2014.

66. "http://www.ddiworld.com/DDIWorld/media/trend-research/globalleadershipforecast2011_es_ddi.pdf", *Global Leadership Forecast 2011,* access 25 July 2014.
67. *How the Top 20 Companies Grow Great Leaders*
68. *Turn The Ship Around!,* 83.
69. *Tactical Leadership Skills for Business Managers,* 66.
70. *Leadership Primer*
71. "https://www.sec.gov/Archives/edgar/data/1018724/000119312517120198/d373368dex991.htm", *SEC Letter from Jeff Bezos,* accessed 5 February 2015.
72. *Leadership Primer*
73. *Jack Welch Speaks,* 73.
74. *Creating Magic,* 110.
75. *Tactical Leadership Skills for Business Managers,* 88.
76. "http://www.inc.com/laura-montini/marissa-mayer-job-is-to-play-defense.html", *Marissa Mayer: Your Job Is to Play Defense for Your Employees,* accessed 10 April 2014.
77. *Leaders Eat Last,* 165.
78. *Leaders Eat Last*
79. *Ten Leadership Truths*
80. *Leaders Eat Last,* 254.
81. *Creating Magic,* 160.
82. *Principled Leadership in a Time of Crisis*
83. *How to Be a Better Leader*
84. "http://www.forbes.com/sites/erikaandersen/2013/03/16/11-quotes-from-sir-richard-branson-on-business-leadership-and-passion", *11 Quotes from Sir Richard Branson on Business, Leadership, and Passion,* accessed 27 August 2014.

85. "http://www.gallup.com/file/services/176708/State%20of%20the%20American%20Workplace%20Report%202013.pdf", *State of the American Workplace,* accessed 21 July 2014.
86. *Leadership Primer*
87. *The Encyclopedia of Leadership,* 451.
88. *Turn The Ship Around!,* 91.
89. *Leadership Primer*
90. "http://fortune.com/2015/06/23/know-your-millennial-co-workers", *Everything you need to know about your Millennial co-workers,* accessed 14 December 2017.
91. *Creating Magic,* 188.
92. "https://mbaonline.pepperdine.edu/resources/infographics/the-importance-of-millennials-in-the-workplace", *The Importance of Millennials in the Workplace,* accessed 14 December 2017.
93. "https://www.bloomberg.com/news/articles/2013-06-06/costco-ceo-craig-jelinek-leads-the-cheapest-happiest-company-in-the-world", *Costco CEO Craig Jelinek Leads the Cheapest, Happiest Company in the World,* accessed 18 August 2014.
94. *Leaders Eat Last,* 134.
95. *Jack Welch Speaks,* 63.
96. *Creating Magic,* 77.
97. *Jack Welch Speaks,* 141.

About the Author:

Gary's life started in turmoil from an early age which can be read in his book, *God's Story: A Foster Child's Story*. He always found positives in life growing up, even though he didn't have a normal childhood. Gary started his leadership experiences as a Sophomore in college as the campus President of the Collegiate YMCA. After not doing well initially in college (too much fun), he went Active Duty Army where he excelled as a leader, and he raised through the ranks to Sergeant as well as graduating Distinguished Honor Graduate of his Primary Leadership Development Course. He returned to finish college after serving in the Army. Over the past 25 years, Gary has held many different leadership roles, is considered a P.P.S. (Professional Problem Solver) and has always been respected by his staff and superiors as a strong and positive leader.

Gary is the author of 3 books; *God's Story: A Foster Child's Story*, *Modern Leadership: A Companion Guide for Today's Leaders* and *How to Create & Understand Facebook Ads Simplified: A Step-by-Step Guide*.